A King Is Born

A KING IS BORN

You are that King

Hopeton K Bailey

Editor: Orville McTaggart

Co-editor: Adain Bailey

authorHOUSE®

AuthorHouse™
1663 Liberty Drive
Bloomington, IN 47403
www.authorhouse.com
Phone: 1-800-839-8640

First published by AuthorHouse   10/17/2011

ISBN: 978-1-4670-0115-1 (sc)
ISBN: 978-1-4670-0116-8 (hc)
ISBN: 978-1-4670-0117-5 (ebk)

Printed in the United States of America

CONTENTS

Acknowledgement

My years of formal schooling started a year earlier than normal. One Monday morning I saw my sisters and brothers going to school and I jumped the fence and went with them without my parents knowing. They looked for me for a long time but could not find me. It was only in the evening when I went back home with my sisters and brothers they knew where I was. My teacher 'Sister Patsy' passed by my house and told my parents that I did very well and she thought I am ready for school. For this reason I want to specially thank her for being my first teacher, one who believed in my potential.

It doesn't matter the amount of work I did for my father I should not be tired. Sometimes my loving mother Ethel Bailey used to be so sympathetic and say, "leave him 'man' the boy must be tired," my father would say, 'what has he done to be tired,' even if I had just carried water on my head from the moon. This however instilled in me that tiredness is a state of mind. For this reason I want to thank my late father Stanley Bailey who instilled so many life changing and character building principles, in me. He taught me that when the going gets rough the tough gets going.

I also want to thank my editor Orville Mactaggart who is an inspiration to me in so many ways although he is always saying that I am the one who inspires him. This inspires me even more.

Finally I must dedicate this book to my love triangle which means everything to me, the love of my life, my children and I. Everything about my children tell me they are stars I see star qualities in their eyes. I must specially mentioned Taifa Bailey who gave me a commandment that I had to follow. This is a covenant just between us.

Finally I also must thank my work colleagues who supported me in some ways and showed me love and appreciation.

INTRODUCTION

A—is for all things are possible when you believe. I f your mind can conceive it you can achieve it. In this book you will see many ways how people before and now achieve great heights by believing in their potential which in fact is unlimited. This potential has been placed in us from creation.

K—is for keeping your eyes on the prize. In my many years of research I have discovered many important facts. One such fact is that I should always keep my eyes focussed on my prize. Keep my goals near and dear to my heart. My inner eyes will go in search of all that I need to make my dreams come true. It is my aim in this book to help you to keep your eyes on that prize.

I—is for the all-important word which you must make it manifest in you and become a part of you. Live this word. I—is for inspiration. This book will instil in you all you need to be inspired to achieve all you set out to achieve and more. You will shock yourself.

N—is for never giving up no matter the circumstances. Remembering that your circumstances are not your life it is just a phase that will teach you lessons to make you stronger. Many people have been in relationships and have been through many storms have life. I asked the question, 'are you still alive.' If you can manage to survive these storms this is true testament to the kind of material that makes you. A king is born. Believe in your strength.

G—is for greatness. Life is for the purpose of expressing yourself through greatness. Gear up yourself to be great. It is only in your mind you will find this resident power to be great. Stop looking around, this power is already in you. What if you were the father of mathematics or the father of science wouldn't you be great. This power is in you from creation. Claim this power and move into your greatness. A king is born.

I—is for inner heights. Be a man within. A king is born.

S—search your heart see what you need to let go. Let go all that is holding you back and making you heavy. Free you mind by freeing up your heart. Make your heart light as a feather.

Born—You must be born again to be a king. This rebirth will take place in your mind when you complete reading my book, 'A king is Born.' This book will remind you, as a matter of fact bring you back to creation when it was said let us make man. We were there everything is in us from that creation day.

The 'everything is possible feeling' reveal itself to us on many occasions. This must be taken seriously and must be developed to a mastery level.

Chris my brother who was never the best at football but he lived moments of this 'everything is possible feeling.' He got five minutes in a game for his football club in a very important match. His coach told him in so many words that he was going on to stay at left back and he should not go forward and that he should leave the attacking option to another player. With five minutes left in the game and his side desperately needed a goal to win. He thought differently and has such the 'everything is possible feelings' took him over. The very first time he touches the ball he gave the ball to a midfielder and ran down the left side with great speed. The ball was played back to him he powered passed two players and made a perfect square to his team mate who elegantly fired the ball into the back of the net. The important goal came. His coach who watched this unfold was furious all the time he was running away from his position. When the goal scored all he could say is that 'look he got a goal'. The 'everything is possible feeling' is real make it real in your life and live magic life. My book A King is Born will make this happen in your life.

I AM THE WAY

BY HOPETON K BAILEY

Here are some simple but important questions that you must answer before you read my book to achieve the fullness.

Who is a King?

Which present day King and which ancient day King do you know much about and what do you know about them?

Can all men be kings?

Would you like to be a King?

What do you have to do to be a king?

Who would you be if you were the father of psychology, Sociology, Science or Mathematics?

Come and journey with me now as I instil the teachings of "The higher One. I will elevate your life to heights you have not been before or otherwise would be. Remember, he who seeks knowledge begins with humbleness.

It's your world and mine. You have your world and I have mine. You have been battered and bruised. You had perilous times. You have been in and out of relationships. Your relationships have been high, low and everything there is between. Life has been a pain to you from the day you have entered this earth. There seems to be no way out. Everything you try failed. I am a failure is your affirmation. Are you still alive? Do you still have life breath? A King is born.

If you have been through so much and you still remain alive and sane, this is testament to the material that makes you. You are a strong person. A king is born. You have all the qualities of a King. You have endurance and you have strength of character. Do you know that you are a King? That is all that you need to move forward. The next time you encounter a negative situation, make a firm affirmation to yourself that you would approach it as a king. When you are in a crisis, think carefully what a king would do. You need to see yourself as one of the greatest kings and work your way out. You live in a world filled with failings because you are looking at yourself as a failure. You see yourself descending at all times and your eyes continue to lead you into this direction. Visualise yourself on a higher level and everything will become one with your vision. You must visualise yourself to the top. Create in your mind that image of a king and live as a King. Man was created to master his world. He has all in his power to harness the forces of nature and create for himself and his people a magnificent kingdom second to none.

GENESIS

When God said let us make man I was there. When I was facing some challenges with some topics in mathematics, I went to visit a king and he told me that my biggest challenge was not with mathematics. He told me that my problem was my state of mind. He said that in the beginning of creation there was the word. When the father of creation came and said "let us make man," I was there. I am the word. I was there from the beginning of creation and I am the creator. I am the creator and I am that I am. All knowledge is in me and in me there is all knowledge. I am a part of all creation because I am the creator. I am the creator and I am in all things. There is nothing that I cannot understand because I am the father of understanding. There is nothing that I cannot apply because I am the father of application. I was there at the beginning of creation of all things because I am the creator. I am one with the word. A king is born.

One must stop saying that he can't understand how to do things because he was there at the creation of all things. When you see that you were there from the beginning of creation because you are the creator, then you will realize that nothing is greater than your level of understanding. When one stops looking up to things, you will change dramatically. Your performance will greatly improve because if you have problems with computers, just remember that at the creation of computers, you were there. If you face a challenge learning any language, just remember you created all language. At the beginning of creation I was there. All things are within because a man is a man. At the beginning of creation, the word was "let us make man."

The man today is the man at the beginning of creation and will be the man forever. Not all men know this. Some men will only be the man of today because they are not enlightened. When you become enlightened and edified, you will be able to disseminate enlightenment to all those around you and this is what will give people a sense of mental freedom. Those of you who have challenges or struggle with anything, remember that you are not struggling with an opponent, but you are struggling only because you don't know who you are. Can a butcher struggle to kill a pig? Can a footballer struggle to kick a ball? Can a cricketer struggle to bold a ball? You only struggle because you don't know who you are. A king is born. You are the creator. You are the creation and you are the word. In the beginning was the word. Enlightenment is therefore for all to receive, but not all will. It is said that many are called but few are chosen. The choice to be one of the chosen few is left up to you. Make the choice and be enlightened. I am in all things. A king is born.

I Control Time

Jacob did not do very well in high school and at the end of year eleven he went to another high school but this time he started from year ten. I was at the same high school that Jacob went to initially and my friends and I thought he was very silly. He is wasting so many years of his life in school. He must be crazy we thought. He however was under the influence of the higher one the father of light. Had spoken to him and instil the principle in his mind that I control time. Jacob set himself some targets and at the end of year eleven he had grades A in all the subjects he took which were what he needed to go onto University. He went on to be a successful lawyer and a renowned politician. I, having experienced this still did not get the concept of I control time. I left high school and was struggling but through persistence I eventually got a job as a pre-trained teacher. While I was at this school teaching I was doing very well and showed the prospects of an outstanding teacher. My students loved me and as such they loved my lessons and this motivated them to excel. I was nearing the end of my contract when Rastaman came to the school to teach and we became friends. He always tried to instil in me the fact that I am an excellent teacher but I am not a teacher until it's on paper. By this he meant I need to go to university and get my degree in teaching. I told him on several occasion that three years out of my life is going to be wasted and this is definitely too long a time for me to give up. He really wished me well and saw the potential in me. I can remember he said to me that 'if a position arise in the school even though you might be the one suited for it based on your ability you would not get it because of your lack of qualification'. This had an effect on me for a while but that was it an effect but not the sort of effect to convinced me to go. I can remember that my time came to an end but I was re-appointed because of my excellent working attitude and abilities. My Rasta friend kept on motivating me to go and get my qualification. He was getting stronger and stronger in his faith. I suspected that he met up with the father of light one night, as he came to me one morning early at school, as we always reach school early in the morning and use the time to reason and develop new ideas for the students, all were aimed at developing their communication and reasoning skills. That morning he said to me 'Bailey you really need to go to university and get your qualification in teaching' as usual I said 'the time is my problem'. This was not like the usual time when we had these conversations because this time he was sent by the father of light. He said to me 'I control time'; Rasta man control time, the time you think is going to be too long is going to be too short'. I am sure this was a direct message from the higher one for this moment was so special I have never heard anything like this before and as such I did not know what to say. The level of message brought me under conviction and consequently I was now ready to go and get my qualification. I was accepted for about three universities. I ended up attending the one that he went to.

My University years were the most loved era of my life and at the end of it although there is really no end to it because, because of those years I will be a perpetual students, I cried when I was supposed to leave. I did not graduate because I could not contain myself and emotion to do so. It was as though I lost a special friend. The time was too short. I must be honest that during my time at this particular university I did not remember what my friend told me until one day I sat on a wall a few days before my time was up, and I saw some fresh men walking pass me and they were discussing their future plans in the university and one of them look at me and said 'I hope I get your room when you leave, you are my icon'. At this point I burst out in tears. Obviously I did not do this so that they could see but I am being honest the tears came rolling down. At this point the words of my friend came back to me and then I realised that this was true. I control time. Rasta man control time. I know most of you reading my book you are at that point in your life when you need to go and get your qualification. You need to go and get your first degree, your masters, or maybe your PHD but you are at that stage where I was years ago stressing about time. I want to instil in you that, 'the I control time.' Time will be too short instead of what you think, too long. Just start. A king is born.

MENTAL EROSION

To a farmer the washing away of soil particles is something devastating and as such he has to take measures to guard against this. The learnt farmer will make contours, barriers and so on to prevent the washing away of soil particles something that is classified as soil erosion. Some people who classified themselves as teacher but they have not met with the father of light they do exactly this, they wash away mental particles. They are agents of mental erosion. When a talent, a gift to the universe is entrusted under your care you must do everything in your powers to ensure that this gift is nurtured and the potential is develop to its maximum. Long gone are the days when one should stick to the design curriculum where day in day out the teacher is dictating to the student and telling the students what is what with no room for students to discover and research and to develop their potential. All students have their innate abilities and talent these abilities and talents must be identified and nurtured.

I have learnt about the boy tapping on the table in his lesson who was several times punished for disrupting lessons. This was a typical time waster who was going nowhere some teachers considered until he was discovered by a science teacher who realised that the boy was investigating the effect that tapping has on different solid, and liquid substance. The boy left his school has one of the most accomplished science students and went on to excel in science at university level. Can you imagine the level of mental erosion that would have taken place if this student was not met by a master teacher? A king is born. I say put an end to mental erosion.

Inevitable we have all played our part in mental erosion. We have washed away the potential mental cells of our students, our child /children and in some way we have made them less than they would have otherwise be. I can put my hand up in this arena as I have been a part of this. Most of the times this is done to protect are to confine to the system in which we operates. This however is no excuse for mental erosion. Find the gift and talents in our young ones and do everything in our powers to develop and nurture them to reach their maximum potential. The father of light has taught us that we should be creative in whatever we do. Create opportunities so that mental potential can be developed. We are all creation, we were made to create. A king is born.

SELF RESPECT— GET SOME OF THAT.

I have heard people complaining on several occasions that they are not getting the respect they deserve from other people. They are not being appreciated. They are not been loved by other people. This seems to knock their feeling and their confidence. Most people feel empowered to the degree to which they are respected and appreciated and loved by other people. While this is true and is really important for your strength to move forward and to elevate your mind to great heights. How much do you respect yourself is the big question? Self-respect get tons of that. A king is born. You don't need to by this at the store or you don't need to do massive search or research to find self-respect. It is all in you respect yourself.

Do you really respect yourself? For if you respect yourself you would not have done the things that you have done. For if you hold yourself in high esteem you would not have done the things you have done. Think about all the great performers that you know or that you have met and you will see that it is the respect that they have for themselves and the concept that they have of themselves that propels them not the respect that people have for them. The respect that people have for them will come and continue to grow but this is only after they have developed and lived with that respect for self. Hold yourself in high esteem and the mass will hold you in high esteem. Have tons a respect for yourself and the mass will have tons of respect for you as well. For in everything you do you are powered by that concept of self. How much you respect and value yourself as a singer will influence your performance. When you sit with a person and they ask you to sing if you start thinking about the fact that person holds you in a very low esteem as a singer or that the person has no respect for you as a singer then you will sing to that level and hence your performance be marred by the other person perception of you. The other person respect for you in that field should not influence you if you want to build self. Self has to be built by self. A king is born. Respect yourself. Value your ability in all areas. Take the time to prepare before you perform. For all activities that you do is a performance that is on the world stage. The world is looking at you. Everything has to start within and not without. Don't look for respect if you have none for you. I respect myself should be your affirmation this should be the very breath that you breathe. The next time you have a presentation to make you should affirm yourself that I am the best presenter. The last time I met and spoke to the father of light is expressions were so clear and precise. He expressed himself so clear. I walk away from the meeting feeling that the higher one has so much respect for himself as a presenter I could feel it. I had no choice but to glow and wallow in that respect flow. Find that river of respect and swim in it all your life. When someone is in your presence they will automatically be emerge in that river and without been given a choice they will respect you. Every single thing you do must be flowing in that river of respect. Keep the river flowing get people to swim in your river. A king is born.

I remember a story from the great book when a king had a sickness. He went to see a prophet to get healed. The prophet looked at him and said, 'you are already healed go to that Small River and dip a certain amount of time and you will be cleaned of all your illness.' The king looked at him and said, I have passed so many great rivers and you want me to dip in such a small river what manner of prophet are you'. Eventually he went and he dipped in the suggested river and he was cleared of all his skin illness. The point I am making your surrounding don't have to be great, you don't have to have the greatest rivers, the greatest luxuries, but your river once it is appointed and anointed by the father of light then people will swim in it and be made whole. Keep your rivers of respect flowing at all times. Respect yourself it is the greatest respect of all. A king is born.

My only school uniform that I had to wear to school was washed every day and iron by my mom. Each morning I stepped out feeing new. I sure there were other students with five uniform so they were able to wear one each day, which was good if you could afford it. I however, won many competitions for well-kept students during my school years even though I had only one uniform. My one pair of shoe when I could afford to wear one was always clean and shine. I wallowed in the river of respect. Respect what you have appreciate it and work with it to keep your river flowing. Each day you could cut yourself with the sharpness of my seam on my trousers. My mom spends the time to use home-made starch to make the seams in my trousers very profound. Other student tried to follow my trend to the point wee they went to the tailor to get their seam stitched in. If I was complaining that I only have one uniform and looking at the other students with their luxuries then I would have dried up my river of respect at no one would respect me because there was no river of respect for them to swim in when they come around me. Conversely because I respected my uniform so much my river which was not the most luxurious of rivers but it was flowing under the anointing and hence people wallowed in it and was enriched. A king is born. Make your river of respect flow so people can wallow in it.

ARE YOU LONELY

I am never lonely for the wind; the rain and the sunshine are my best friend. A king is born. For he who seeks friendship in man to keep them from loneliness will at sometimes be lonely. I treasure every moment I spend with people. I appreciate the level of communication that all human share. This is of course is very important and cannot be taken lightly. Loneliness must be controlled so too boredom if one is going to be a King. In order to excel and soar to great heights, one has to make nature their best friend. Be at peace with nature enjoy the sunshine as much as the rain, play with the bright clouds and sometimes with the dark gloomy ones. A king is born I have added nature to my friend list.

I AM AMONGST
THE LIVING

Why do you search for I amongst the dead I am alive. Let your works project your life. If you give up and have no purpose in life how will you express yourself? You will be living amongst the dead. Stay alive. Find something purposeful to do make it your dream, believe in it and do it with all of your might. The first time I saw Bob singing I learnt a lesson. He had his eyes close. I knew that he was doing it with all his might. He was focussed. This is what we should do find something meaningful to do and do it with all our might. A king is born. Some people think they know me, some people even paint their own picture of me, and some people even try to create a picture of me to project to the world. I say to you I am amongst the living. I am alive. I am creating, I am learning, I am adapting, I am flexible.

A Boy Who Changed
A Community

I grew up in a very peaceful rural community. It was so peaceful that the sound of gunshots was very rare and strange to us. If someone in our community got robbed or shot, it would be the talk of the community for months and even years, if the victim had succumbed to injuries and died. Life was very simple for us. We did not have access to many luxurious things, but we were happy because we all shared what we had in a fun loving way. With the sale of lands and the migration of other people from other places, our community changed when a village was created adjacent to our community. This village was dominated by people who fled from the capital city to take up residence in our community. They brought with them a myriad of attitudes, values and cultures, but most regrettably, they brought with them violence. I called this new community the Ghetto.

The sounds of gunshots became more regular and it soon became the norm. The community had lost its true spirit and culture. There became segregation between our community and the ghetto. There were also the occasional clashes between us and them. In retrospect, I must admit though that there were several very good and genuine people who lived in that ghetto. As time passed, I had formed relationships and had some very good friends that lived there and I even had some fun times hanging out in the ghetto. As the anti-social behaviours escalated, the ghetto got worse and the security forces had to be brought in to prevent and reduce the level of violence that was perpetuated in the community. It became a battle field.

One day, there came a ray of hope. A very educated boy who attended one of the most prestigious traditional high schools in the capital city came to live in our community. For some strange reason, this boy came and totally fell in love with the people in the ghetto. In reality, he spent most of his time in the ghetto. I have been there with him on many occasions. The people from the ghetto also fell in love with him an as such, they really appreciated his company and his teachings. A king is born. As time passed, the boy and I had several discussions on how we would, should or could merge and save both communities. We knew that it would be a very steep uphill battle, but it was imperative that we take action and very fast. Through, hard work, determination and strength of character, the boy started a mission to change the state of the community. With his experience and knowledge of psychology, he first started to change the minds of the people. He organized and formed a community development organization which brought the media to the community and he also promoted several activities to revive and keep the community spirit alive. Among the many activities that he organized were football competitions and educational assistance. One of the most remembered activities that occurred was when he brought the media to one of his football competitions and the players, spectators and the entire community were able to see themselves on television. With our world now in the Information Age, the whole world now knew about this community.

The community continued to grow over time and there is now a friendly rivalry between the different villages in the community. A king is born. This boy has brought the communities together and has also removed the negative stigma that was once associated with the community. This has done wonders for the community as adults and even the elderly are now coming out to support the games. The level of discipline has vastly improved because of the support given by the elders in the community. Through this initiative, many of the youngsters are now motivated to improve their lives in a positive way. This boy has through mentoring and teaching the youths, especially the ones 'on the corners' have encouraged many of them to stay in school. A king is born. I was once told that if each man heals another man, all men would be healed and if you can heal a man you are not just a man, you are kingly character. This boy has not only healed a man but he has healed an entire community. He is a king.

It is in all of us to be able to stand up and make a positive contribution to life and to make our communities better. When everyone stands up for a good cause, the world will become one big community with one good community spirit. This is the global village we are dreaming of. The power that you have in you should not be taken lightly. It should be nurtured and used for a good cause. It should be used to heal others. Leading people in the right direction and developing their lives positively without having access to the many luxuries of the world is an act that is coming from the light in us. This is an act from the father of light. When the father of light resides in you, all you can do is act as a light because you are of the light. You are the light. A king is born. The darker the room, the brighter your light will shine. Don't be put off or put down by the darkness. When the situations that you are trying to change look very bad and there seems to be no hope, just remember that the darker the room the brighter your light will shine. It is important to remember that the situation will increase in darkness if no one stands up and shine their light. The people who are courageous enough to stand up and shine their lights are the type of kings that the world needs. Create or do something positive that will turn on an orbit forever. Let it become the culture of the society to the point where it has to take a major phenomenon to change it. A king is born

RELATIONSHIPS

I KNOW MUCH ABOUT RELATIONSHIP AS MUCH AS YOU KNOW

Most things will work when the people involved have one common objective. Although some may take other routes to get there, they are working toward the same target or goal. Some relationships have no objective or target, and as such, there is no direction. This is sometimes the source of what causes problems. Because there is no clear directions, people don't know where they are going, and if you don't know where you are going, you will led by anyone or anything. There are times in a relationship when one party is giving their all and the next party is not. Party A does any and everything to make the relationship work and to make ends meet. Party B, on the other hand, can be very nonchalant. This will lead party A to a high level of frustration. In situations like this, party A usually stop putting effort in the relationship. When this occurs, Party B usually tends to realise that the relationship is turning sour and start putting 100% in to keep it going. If Party A is not careful, the same nonchalance may occur in their relationship cycle. Party A might realise that Party B is exerting this effort and start thinking it is payback time. The thought in Party A's mind might be that "when I was giving my all you did not respond positively so I am going to do the same to you and I don't care." Once this occurs, then Party B will get frustrated also and stop caring about the relationship. This usually causes a cycle which will continue until the relationship crashes or a major catastrophe occurs.

Positive things usually will not occur unless Party A and Party B start working towards the same common goal. This is called "Greatship" instead of relationship. This occurs when the engine plays its role and the captain guides the ship safely to the harbour. When each party play their role and play their role to the fullest, this will ensure the survival of a relationship or to convert a relationship into a "Greatship". My friend once told me that a boy went to a girl and said "I like you and I think you like me too." Before the girl could answer he said to her "anyway let's not start a relationship because that is too big for me, let's start a "Relation—boat." In retrospect, I discovered that the key to any relationship is to start from the basic principles although these principles may look seem or childish. These basic principles include knowing or having an understanding of what each party likes and dislikes. Once this is known and understood, then, finding common grounds is a key to keeping the relationship alive. Both parties must find things to do together. They must create things that both of them love to do and find pleasure in doing it. The more they continue to do this, the more they want to be together. They must find movies that both of them love to watch and spend time to watch them. They must find places that both like to go and go there. This will bring the bond in the relationship.

FATHER OF THEM ALL

If you were the father of psychology, the father of philosophy, the father of medicine, the father of sociology, the father of science, the father of music, the father of humour, or the father of mathematics, how would the world see you? Without a doubt, the world would see you as a king. You are a king. You are the father of these disciplines. It is in us all. We were created with all this knowledge. It is in all of us. All things are the manifestation of the father of light and the father of knowledge. Man is the ultimate manifestation of the father of knowledge. All things are in us. A king is born. If we should walk around the earth inside out and outside in, what difference would there be between us. We would all be displaying the same organs and system. A king is born. You are a king. Get up, stand up, and stand up for your position. What is your position? What is your place? Your place is ultimately determined by you. You are in charge of all of this.

You should never traverse the universe under the impression of other men. You should write and live your own script and your own theories. Live the life of a king. A king is born. You must see all things, hear all things, understand all things and master all things. If you were the father of humour then you could make the world laugh any time you want. You could make everyone laugh themselves to tears if you want to. You could create happiness in everyone's' heart. The power to change bad situations with moments of laughter and moments of happiness would be yours. This is what the world needs. The world needs people with great sense of humour who can change bad situations into memorable ones. Strive to be the father of humour. Be the one the world needs. Be the one who can make people happy by just thinking about you. It is all in you. It is just a choice you have to make. If you make this choice and think carefully about it and then create the discipline to elevate yourself up to the level, with faith in yourself, you will get there. You will master this important aspect of life. A king is born. You can make people happy. Imagine yourself walking into a room filled with people who are all sad and your very presence instantly changes the complexion of the room from sadness to a room glowing with happiness.

You have the power to relieve people of their stress and frustration. I am sure you are all aware that when people are stressed and frustrated they get emotional and emotions have a way of making people make stupid decisions. Stress usually causes stupidity to outshine logical thinking. A king is born. You are the one who is able to stand in the meeting room and ease the pain, the stress, the strain and make people relax and think logical. I am the father of humour. I am able to generate laughter in the hearts of men. I am able to make people feel happy. I will help people to live healthier and happier and maintain good relationships with others. I have always asked myself this question "'why is it ok for you to be serious with yourself but it is not ok to laugh with yourself?" People will think you are insane if you are seen laughing with yourself but if you are serious with yourself it seems to be ok. Is it healthier to laugh or to be serious? Which one of these activities supports or enhances life and happiness? I am sure you will agree with me that most people tend to spend more time being serious than what is spent laughing. I have realised that we have evolved into becoming machines that will self-destruct. At the extreme, it is as if we are committing suicide. One has a choice to be happy or sad. Laugh all you want because the more you laugh, the more you will draw closer to the father of humour.

I have created a life of laughter and happiness by making my own jokes and laughs at them. Laughter should be a daily exercise. One should make the effort to think consciously about laughing and just laugh. Once you try it, you will soon start laughing naturally and you will see how this will chase anger, stress and frustration away. Frustration, anger and negative emotion has no place in the heart of happy people. If your house is not clean, the father of light cannot enter. Anger and negative emotions will keep your heart dirty. Let them go, laugh them off, say good bye to them and your heart will become cleaner. A king is born. I can laugh. I can maintain my calm. In a raging storm, the fathers of light's followers were panicking because they did not know what to do because he was sleeping. When he arose he uttered, "Peace be still." Did he panic? No he maintained his calm. Maintain your calm at all times. The more you do this, the more you will master it, thus the more you will be raised to the heavens. Even in the face of war be calm. Never panic.

Be entirely psychological. Know the psychology of all things and all people and of all organisations. Know the psychology that makes you a "larger than life character". A king is born. If you were the father of psychology, you would be closer to the father of light. You would be a son of the light. What makes people tick? What makes an organisation 'click'? What makes the world go round? Make the most of these questions. Find the answer and blow them as far as possible out of proportion. To find out what makes people 'tick' is your goal. This will put you in control. You will become the one that everybody will come to. You will be the "go to man." A king is born. Be the "go to man." Be the father of all psychology. If people want to run, make them run. If they want to laugh, make them laugh. If they want to have fun make them have fun. If they want to think, make them think. Be the father of psychology. Be the man who makes people think. If they want to lose their fear, let them lose their fear. If they want to live magic lives, let them live magic lives. Be the father of psychology. If your organisation want to raise achievements or raise recognition or establish personal goals, make them do it. Find the solution and lead this change. Spend sleepless nights until this happens. The world will gravitate to positive energy. Make it happen and be calm and diligent about it. If at all possible, be as easy going as much. If you do this with little ease, people will be able to think that you have more in reserve. Create an impact. This lasting impact will rest in the minds of people forever.

Be the father of psychology. When people don't see you, their hearts must grow fonder. They must miss you. They must want to hear from you. They must think they are missing out on something. This is the impact you must have on the world. You are the father of psychology. Create an impact that is "larger than life". If people around you are living in fear, try to alleviate their fears because fear will damage and limit performance. Let them see the result of working without fear. Always strive to free people of their fears. Drive their fears away and let them live meaningful lives. Most people have a level of fear that they have learnt during their past that prevents them from performing and living life to the fullest. Be the father of psychology. Free them like a bird out of its cage. Find out what motivates each man to free himself and assist him in a way that he will have no choice but to accept it. Oceans can be dried up at the sound of your voice or large seas can be part in two halves by the stretching of your arms. It is all in you, be the father of psychology. Bless the nation with power to overcome all fears and you will be close to the father of light. A king is born.

WE ALL ARE ONE

I have envisioned all human beings walking inside out and outside in. What we will see is organs and systems. Apart from that, we will all look the same. We all are one. So the big question is, what makes us different? I know that what we think makes us different. Our life and our being is the ultimate manifestation of the father of light. We are the manifestation of knowledge. The more we know, the closer we are drawn to the father of light. We have to be able to visualise and conceptualise. The differences that we see among men are differences that are created, but in essence, we all are one. We all make use of the same big tank of oxygen. According to Rastafarian culture, principle and language we all are one. This can be shown by their usual responses such as "yes I." In addition, they will say "I and I" instead of saying you and I. You and I put both parties on two different levels, two different viewpoints or two different perspectives. When I and I is used, there is no difference between the two parties. We all are one. All men are kings. Normally when you say "you," for example, "you boy sit down," there is a message behind it. It's a strong language. It is suggesting something is wrong or someone is below par. In retrospect, the sound of the word "I" make one feels "high". I and I is the way forward. This puts all men on the same level.

Why should I separate myself from the next person? I and I represent a language of power, a language which puts us all on the same level. A king is born. It is by respecting one's inner most self and understanding the concept of the inner self that one will be able to conceptualise the higher level. The inner height is therefore for us to attain. It's the attainment of this inner height that will take you to the place where you will see all men as equal. Find and sustain respect for all creation and you will be able to respect each other as one. Try to observe some of the world's most powerful men. They usually think carefully about what they say or do because they know that what they say or do will be highly scrutinised. They know that they have to show respect to all men or they will lose their credibility or fame. The light within you is bright so you must see this light within you and shine it through. Shine it through as bright as possible, so others around will be able to see this light. When they see this light, they will be motivated to turn their lights on as well. I have met many people who are in high places, but are they really Kings? Some say that they are and people say they are but when you listen carefully and look at their actions, they seem to be a very shallow within. We need to develop the light within each of us. This will light up the world. It is the fire within that keeps us alive. Light up your heart and grow.

SAY MOVE MOUNTAINS— SAY MOUNTAINS GET OUT OF MY WAY

A king is born. Everybody thinks their burden is the heaviest. If one should think that they are the only one under stress and that their burden is the heaviest, think again. Stress will always be in our lives, but the greatest thing is how you deal with it. How you react is important. How you perceive your stress will affect how you react to it. If you convince yourself that this is just another challenge for which you have the solution, you have perceived victory; hence you will react accordingly to that perception. I have always heard that the best words to use when situations are at their extreme worst are the magic words "the father of light loves me as one of his special children, so he will not give me more than what I can bear".

You were given power and dominion over all the earth. It is written that the earth is the Lord's and the fullness there of. Also remember that in the beginning there was the word and the word was with the father of light and the word was the light. All power is in the word. All things start from the thought and then the word has to be spoken for things to come into being. Say "move mountain." A king is born. If I should tell you that you are going to live your life without having testing times or challenges, you would stop reading my book and never read any more of my books again. Life is filled with challenges. This is what makes life exciting and that is what separates ordinary people from Kings, that is, how we deal with our challenges. We need to stop running to the rock because the rock will one day look somewhere to run to. You are the rock. All things and power is within you. Perceive your challenges as a puzzle that can be solved and you are the solution. Say "move mountain". There are going to be times when the challenges are so great that even when you say "move mountain" you will still see the mountain standing firm in your way. I suggest that you say "Mountain get out of my way."

I have seen massive floods, severe earthquakes and tsunamis in my lifetime. They have certainly made things move and as such, had a massive impact on lives. A king is born. The power of the word in you is much greater than all these forces. These forces of nature can be harnessed by you and be put to great use. This is the intention of the father of light. When we start using the forces of nature to good use, we are living in the heavens. Mastering this divine power should be our aim. At this point, when you say "move mountain" the mountain will move. Believing without doing is of no use, and as such, no change and no success will be had. You have to act. It is not for you just to say "move mountain" and expect the mountain to suddenly disappear. You have to think carefully, design a winning strategy, then apply the strategy carefully and tactfully, and then the mountain will start to crumble. Once the mountain starts to crumble, then the mountain is showing signs that it is getting weaker while you are getting stronger. Attack again, but this time double your force and the already shaken mountain will finally move.

Some make the mistake of lessening their force when they see that the mountain is starting to crumble, thus allowing the mountain to regain strength and get back to normal. At this point we tend to give up because we say the mountain will not be moved. The successful removal of one mountain will give you a degree that no university on earth can give. This qualification comes straight from the father of light. This is your pass to enter into his gates. Do so with thanksgivings and praise. Now you are able to, you are confident to move several other mountains. Do not be weakened if in the future you try to move a mountain and it takes a longer time than expected. Just remember that life is like that at times and time is the master. Teaching others to move mountain will bring you closer to the divine.

Every time you are in the business of making people's life better, success will bring you closer to the divine. Remember we are here to serve. A king is born.

Every King has a duty to care for his people. Serve as much as you can. Protect and serve humanity to the best of your ability because the more you do this, the closer you draw to the divine. I am looking forward to see you in the heavens. A king is born. The world is a challenging place. If it were not so, then it might be boring for some. Face your challenges and be happy about your achievements. Your success will be a lesson for another generation. Let them say "like a fruit in due season, that's how you came." They must often time say "if it was not for you, how we would have found the solution to this." Like a fruit in due season, that's how you came. A king is born. I know some people will say that they are trying to move mountains for a long time and nothing has been happening but be patient because patience is a virtue. Samson was blind but he was smart enough to tell someone to lead him to the pillars of the kingdom so when the time was right he could push the kingdom down. He put himself in the right position at the right time. Where or what is your position? When are you going to say "move mountain?" People will say that you are a coward if you run away from your mountains. Don't be afraid of that. If you need time to prepare and you have to run, don't just run, but put on wings and fly. Prepare yourself, gain strength and then move that mountain out the way. Win your battles by choosing your words and your time carefully. A king is born. Remember the duty of a king is to serve. What mountains are you moving today?

You Will Not Be
A King By Surprise

I have met several persons who have fantasies for nice cars and other luxurious things. I am sure that you have met some as well. I was in awe when one of my friends told me that he wanted to own a Bentley. He was not from a wealthy family but he had done very well in school. He had a good job working as a Bank Teller. He was different from anyone I have ever met because his passion to own this car was very different. He spoke about the car as if it was a person. He once found a picture of his dream car on his computer (internet) and used it as his computer screen saver. Before he goes to bed at night, he spoke to the car saying "baby I love and I'll you see you tomorrow." As soon as he awakes in the mornings, he would say "good morning, baby I love you and I hope you had a good night." This is a passion that I have never seen before. The car became a part of his life. He was fully focused and determined that he would own this car. This has proven to me that whatever you think or perceive in your conscious mind can come to reality. He now owns a Bentley. Having experienced this, I now have pictures of some deprived children from several countries as my computer screen saver. I have deep thoughts of helping these children. I often think about creating a better life for them. Some of them are suffering from lack of food, some need wheelchairs and some need financial support to go to school. Whatever their distress is, I always think about helping them. When I am going to bed at nights, I say good night to them as they are my own children. When I wake up in the mornings, I say good morning to them and bless them with my words of power.

I know that at some point in my life I will be able to assist them. Unlike my friend, I would love to own an island where I could build a large house and create a new world of luxury for them. A king is born. Many people are destined to own houses and fancy motor vehicles. While this is good, why not dream of owning an island. The heart of a man is in the things that he loves and dreams of. We must love people not for what we can get from them but for what we can do to make their lives better. As you love, try to pull things in your life with the force of attraction. Use this force of attraction to pull in the power to help a mass of people and to make a difference in their lives. I always say good night to people who are suffering before I go to my bed at nights. Even when I don't look at them on the computer, their images are still in the forefront of mind. They are a part of the force that drives me. They motivate and inspire me to work for success. Any day that I can make a whole nation happy, I will be close to the father of light. This is the work that the father of light intends for us to do. You have this power in you.

Some of you are able at this very stage in your life to start making that difference in the life of a mass of people. You thought that it is in fancy things that you would find true happiness. True happiness is already in you. Create happiness in other people and your happiness will be multiplied. A king is born. Take care of the mass. Create that image in your mind when you walk through the village, and as people see you passing, they will follow you. You will see a domino effect and the whole village will be behind you. If you start to run, they will start to run behind you. A king is born. It is the love that is within you that will ignite this light. It will light your world and the world of others. The person's hand you shook today and took it for granted might be the same hands that will save your life tomorrow. Kings are born every day, today might just be his or your day.

Don't use the past as an excuse to be rebellious. Some people like to be rebellious and so they seek all the possible chances to do it. They will act rebellious even when there is no situation or reasons present for them to do so. When they are confronted, they will reply by saying "I remember what you did." Is the past more important than now? We are having a good time now so why not think about now. Why drag your memory to bad things in the past. There must have been elements of good in the past so why not dwell on the glorious moments. They just want to be rebellious. How do we overcome these threats to enhancing good relationships? Rebellious nature is easy to deal with. It has to be dealt with using reverse psychology. If you are confident in support of the concept of Reverse Psychology, then this will combat the rebellious nature in others. Give them something to rebel about but it must be the opposite of what you want them to do. If you want your partner to talk to you about your job every time that you come from work, just pretend that you don't like your job and the rebellious nature will go to work. Every time you come from work it is sure that you will be asked "How work was today and how was your day?" A King is born.

I am a great teacher. The word education is from the Greek root "Educo" which means to lead out. Hence, when one is truly educated one is led out of darkness. When one steps into the light, one will find all the gifts, talents and abilities that God has embedded in us from creation. As according to Howard Gardner, there are eight intelligences, namely Interpersonal, Intrapersonal, Logical, Linguistic, Naturalistic, Bodily, Spatial and Musical. Man is the manifestation of the father of light with all these levels of intelligence it is in us to raise them to the highest of heights. Gone are the days when one sees someone who is prospering or living a good and successful life and say "I wish I was like that." You are already like that, or in some cases even better. Just find your gifts, talents and abilities and develop them to the fullest. This is not anything difficult to do. Anything you want to do you can achieve. First, all you need to do is to think about the things that you love to do. Once you have done this, and then apply all the positive activities or techniques. A king is born. A new king is born when you realise what you are good at and you build or work on making it better with all your might. God did not bless some people more than others. If that was the case he would be a bias God. He gave everyone talents, abilities and gifts but some people nurture, grow and build on their gifts while others bury their talents and gifts under a tree leaving them for other people find them and take them away.

Luckily for you, there are always more talents in you even when you have squandered or idled some of them away. There is always that continuous source reproducing these talents. You are a shining the star.

You are even greater than the shining star you wish or think you are. How are you going to find this out? Well, if you stay in a corner and hide yourself from the possibilities to shine your light then the light in you would seem meaningless. Remember the words of the powerful song, "This little light of mine, I am going to let it shine." King David played his instrument and sang his troubles away and when the troubles went away, then success comes. Shine your light so all can see. A king is born. A new king is born. Jesus was never afraid to shine his light. He used his words carefully and smartly to protect himself from harm. Remember, his duty was to serve and save lives. When the mob wanted to stone the woman to death, Jesus shone his light. He used words to defeat and overcome the situation. He had put them to the ultimate test by telling them that anyone who is without sin should cast the first stone. Shine your light so all can see. Shine your light to the fullest so others will see your light, and in so, they will learn how to shine their lights as well. It is by you expressing yourself to the fullest that others will be able to free themselves.

You are here for a purpose. If you are not serving your purpose then you are of no good to yourself and others. Serving another purpose might be destroying not only you but destroying others. You need to live your purpose to the fullest. Marcus Garvey preached that life is given for the purpose of expression. A tree expresses itself by the beauty of its leaves, branched and sometimes hanging fruits. A flower expresses itself by the beauty of its bloom. The river expresses itself by way of its flow and meandering. A man should express himself by way of his achievements and deeds. What you achieve will define your purpose. Take a good look at the man or woman in your community who sets out to achieve their goals. You can see them going from one step to the next with success. This is the man or woman to whom everybody goes. This is what your life should be about, one with a plan. Your life is not just for you alone, you need to create life for all around you, and in so doing inherit the earth.

The earth is the lords and the fullness there of. If you create wealth and store it like the ants store food for the rainy season, then your generation will become great. This is what great families and great nations do. Live for or create something to develop wealth for your children and your children's children. There is a thin line between love and hate, so don't be fooled because not everyone will love you and in the same vain, not everyone will hate you. One thing for sure is that you will be respected and everyone will have to accept you for who you are. Live for something. A king is born. Remember at all time that you can't please everybody no matter how hard you try. One law of success is to cement in the back of your mind that not everyone will be pleased by your efforts. This is good for you because it should be a motivating factor to work harder. Remember that everything that happens to you on your journey happened to make you a stronger person. Everything happens for a reason. When you see an obstacle in your way, remember to say "I am a giant killer" and just attack it methodologically. Always expect the unexpected so that nothing can come upon you suddenly. If you don't expected the unexpected you will sometimes fail because you have no plan, and so, you heave to quickly improvise one. Always remember old saying, "If you fail to plan, then you plan to fail." Using the correct method to attack your giants is very important. If you use a method and it works then you can probably use this method all the time. The more you apply this method, the more you will master it. At some point you will be a master of killing your giants. Remember too that men at some point are masters of their faith. Whatever you believe in, you will become a master of it. Believe in your method.

A Man Who Fell Poorly Infront Of KFC.

One day a man who felt very hungry and wanted to eat some Kentucky Fried Chicken did something really smart. He did not have any money so he went in front the restaurant and fell down. As he fell, he started sweating. A large crowd of people then came over and stood over him. A very helpful lady took an orange from her bag and said to the man "Eat this orange and you will be ok." The man who fell down replied "If I had wanted to eat orange I would have done this in front the market. "Can I get some chicken please? the man asked. You can be this kind of desperate person if you want to. The important lesson is if you want the blessing from the father of light you have to put yourself in the right place. Be at the right place at the right time. The art of preparation is a key to success. So many time people are empowered to act and they just act. And because there was no preparation they lost sight of their goal and then the focus and the will power die. This is because there was no planning and preparation. You must create a chart that will inform you what will come next and always have your contingency plan. Let nothing come upon you suddenly. If this happen you will have to improvise a plan and you might not struck upon the correct method required. This might lead to failure and frustration. Always have a plan. A king is born. Remember at all time that you are on a mission for the 'higher one'. The work you are doing is not of yourself but it is the work of the 'Father of light'. When the rain fall it's not just a fall of rain it's the works of the almighty and when the sunshine it's not just the shine of a sun it's the works of the almighty. When I perform a task it's not just a task performed it's the work of the almighty. Everything I do is 'JAH WORKS' I am on a mission. A king is born. People will watch you and fight you and the more they fight you, you get stronger and they wonder what's going on. Can you fight against Jah and win? Let them fight because they are just providing a source of strength. Do you know what you are living for? Are you living for a purpose? If some of us know what we are living for we would not dear to think or do the things we have done. We would not dear to say the things we have said. A purposeful life is so much different from a life without purpose. For if you close a door on a man with a purpose you have just open a million more doors. For a man with a purpose will not sleep until he sees the light and when he sees the light he will be one with the light and it is the light that is the door. This light is like unto millions of doors. To a man with a purpose there is no road block for the light is the road and the light is like unto a million roads. The 'father of light' now ask you, "what is your purpose?" Be thou clever in your endeavours be a king. Simplicity, simplicity, simplicity is what make people be looked at as a king. The good teacher must make the lesson, even though difficult, simple and clear so all the students will understand. The great king must device simple strategy to solve difficult situations.

There is a story which established the prestige and power of an ancient king. Two ladies, lady A and Lady B had two baby boys in a village on the same day. When the ladies went to sleep, lady A's baby died. She woke up before lady B and discovered that her baby had died, she took lady B's baby and gave her the dead baby. In the morning when everyone woke up, there was a big argument over the babies. Lady B knew that it was her baby that was alive and that the dead baby was for lady A. The argument went on for a while until one of the wise men that was passing saw what was happening and took them to the king. The king listened to what they were saying then he thought after having listened their stories, the best way to solve the problem was to kill both babies so both mothers would be on the same level and both could go and have more babies. Lady A was very happy with the decision and she said "Yea, kill the baby, you are a wise king." Lady B said "You are the best king ever but don't kill the baby, give the baby to lady A." At this point lady A showed mixed feelings. She looked both happy and sad but sadness was more dominant. The king now realised that if the baby was truly for Lady A she would not have wanted her baby to be killed. The wise King then said "Give the baby to the good mother, Lady B because she is the actual mother of the baby." A king is born.

Can you read between the lines? Can you read implicit ideas? Simplicity is the best policy. According to Tracy, a lorry fell over and got stuck in a bridge. The owners tried to pull it out with no avail. The police came on the scene and they tried to do the same. They tried pulling the truck with relentless effort but still nothing happened. As they were just about to give up, a little boy came on the scene and looked at what the men were doing. As he looked, he shook his head and said to them, "Let the air out of the tires". They let the air out of the tires and the truck got out as easy as pie. Do you look at simple details or do you try to think too hard at all times? Most of the times the solution you need is right in front your face. Some people will say it is too close for you to see. It is in the blind spot. A king is born. Simplicity is the best policy.

EXPERIMENTAL WORK AS A TEACHER.

This study investigated the effects of students' attitudes towards Mathematics using Mini-Whiteboards as a method of Learning and Teaching strategy in a Secondary School in Lincolnshire, England.

The locus level, attitudes and levels of participation in Mathematics lessons were also investigated. The study adopted pre-test and post-test, with three experimental groups, (two KS4 (A and B)) and one KS3 (C)) and one control group (KS4 (D)). One hundred and twenty students from four purposively selected classes were the subjects. Four instruments were developed:

- Pupils participation in lessons
- Diagnostic testing
- Assessment for Learning (AfL)
- Pupils become active learners.

These were validated and shared with other staff members in the Mathematics department. Findings showed that the correct usage of mini-whiteboards had significant effects on students' attitude towards Mathematics. The participants exposed to the investigation demonstrated an interest in the strategy, expressing and sharing their views by grading lessons on mini-whiteboards. It was concluded that Mathematics teachers should be trained to effectively use mini-whiteboards in the classroom, because the techniques involved are very effective in improving students' attitude and hence performance in Mathematics when combined with the conventional method.

Contextual Statement

I have completed a degree in Combine Studies and also completed my Qualified Teacher Status with the University of Derby. I studied three years full-time at the University of the West Indies, Jamaica to successfully complete a Credit Diploma in Mathematics and Physical Education in 2003.

I came to England in 2006 and started teaching Physical Education. I have taught Mathematics at a secondary school in Lincolnshire. In 2009 I found that this is a school plagued with behavioural issues, only boasting a 'Satisfactory' OFSTED report. Exclusions are very high and attendance, although improving, is still poor. Most of the better students who are successful in their eleven plus examination attended the nearby grammar schools. This can be concluded that the average and below average students attended the school where I work and intend to carry out my study.

The majority of the students showed some level of motivation to learn, however, their aspiration was not to excel to their full potential. About 20% of the student population were not focused on improving their academic performance and at most times were not motivated to participate in the activities during the lessons. This 20%, which is approximately four students in most of the classes, tend to distract the other average learners and cause them to lose focus.

As a Mathematics teacher, I discovered that the majority of the students were not interested in Mathematics and those who showed some interest, did not have the right attitude that would help them to gain an "A-C" grade at GCSE Level. Having used the conventional method of teaching and observed other lessons with teachers using the similar strategies, I am of the opinion that employing a teaching strategy with infectious enthusiasm will motivate students to perform and hence develop a better attitude towards the subject. In this study I used mini-whiteboards in three of my classes in an effort to study its effect on:

- Improving students' participation in lessons
- Enhancing diagnostic testing
- Fostering Assessment for Learning (AfL)
- Helping students to become active learners

I also designed a questionnaire which was given to the students to complete. This questionnaire specifically requested the students' feedback from their Maths lessons. A response box was provided to collect students' questionnaires. This helped me to gain knowledge of the locus of attitude and participation in Mathematics lessons in my classes and other classes as well.

Engagement with the Knowledge Base

According to Donovan (2005; 47) the DFES view is strongly in favour of new materials for teaching and learning. The centralisation of production of materials for teaching and learning rather than just for assessment is often criticised by professionals. The use of mini-white boards is a useful new material instead of the usual workbooks. The conventional method where students' works are done in workbooks is very effective and has proven to be a useful strategy in developing students' academic skills. Workbooks are also important to store useful examples and are great resources for revision and quick research for students, if examples and notes are kept accurately and effectively. Teachers also use workbooks to provide important feedback to students. This formative assessment enables learners to see the level achieved and what they need to do to make progress to the next level. Workbooks are also used to assess learning. This can be effectively done by students completing tasks and the teacher having students exchange books to peer mark. The questions are done on the board by teachers and in some cases students are also requested to do so. This is true for the vast majority of schools.

Alluding to the fact that workbooks are very useful in the aforementioned ways, why is the implementation of new materials imperative? This is because there are cases where students are reluctant to work in their books because of the fear of getting the answer incorrect and that other students will notice their weakness. The implementation of the use of mini-whiteboards will facilitate full class participation and students will be given a chance to display answers in a way that only the teacher can see. Students will do many examples until they are happy to work in their book. In this particular school, where students' attitudes are generally poor, the use of mini-whiteboards provide this opportunity along with a new exciting experience for students.

At the start of a good lesson, the teacher should revisit concepts learnt in previous lessons. Glover and Law (2002; 129) argued that recapitulation is important. They state that students need opportunities to revise their work and to consolidate their learning. Providing questions on worksheets or on the board so students can answer questions in their books is a good way of testing, if students have grasped previous concepts taught, and providing opportunities for consolidation. The teacher will then develop pre-requisite knowledge for the concept that is about to be taught. This is effective teaching. If one is to teach histogram with unequal class interval, frequency density must be found. In a situation where students are given frequency density and class interval, can they find frequency? A good teacher will reinforce or teach the concept of transposition of formula. In other situations where students are asked to find a stratified sample, they must be able to simplify fractions. Giving students' work of this nature to do in their books, as mentioned before, is good and is of paramount importance. The problem though is that the lesson becomes monotonous and lacks excitement. Glover and Law (2002; 129) also argue that the same topic can be taught in two different ways to ensure that learning is complete and that the teacher has recognised the variation in preferred learning styles.

The implementation of mini-whiteboards will eliminate this problem and on the contrary add an exciting start to the lesson. The effective and infectious enthusiastic teacher can write questions on his mini-white board to get students ready and then show them questions. Students are then given one minute. After doing this, the teacher will say "show me," at this point all students will show their results. Students become more involved and play a more active part in the lesson. Students like to be active learners and controlled lessons. In addition, they like to feel safe to perform in an environment where there is a level of consistence and fairness. The teacher is given a vast amount of opportunities to praise the entire class, even if some answers are incorrect. The fact that they participated deserves credit. Mini-white boards do help with diagnostic testing. Praising participation is very vital in improving students' attitude towards Mathematics. It was Glover and Law (2002; 31) that argued that teacher-student relationships are fundamental to effective learning and have been investigated as fundamental to school improvement. They stated that bad relationships mar the learning experience for students. What better way is there to build positive relationships with students than to make them feel good about themselves by praising them?

Assessment for Learning is a major part of every good lesson. The students are asked to provide evidence in their books that they are comfortable answering questions at a particular level. Some students develop a phobia to work in their books because they don't want to have incorrect work in their books. The use of the mini-white board is a useful tool in removing this problem. This can be solved by asking students to work questions out on mini-whiteboards, have it checked by a peer, learning support or the teacher before recording it in books. Students are able to make changes before their work is recorded in books. The majority of work recorded in their books will be of high standard and correct. Their books will now become a very useful resource of reference.

In some lessons that I have taught and that I have observed, the use of the "Stop light" system was employed, this is where students show "red" if they are completely blank on a concept or "orange" if they are nearly there and so on. According to Donovan (2005; 39) on the National Entitlements for learners, all professionals are expected to achieve effective teaching and learning which should be supported by good quality formative assessment. The use of the Stop light strategy is an effective tool in assessing students' progress and providing necessary feedback to learners to help them to make progress.

The negative effect this have is that students do not generally want to put a red card up disclosing openly to whole class that they are struggling. This is the time when they should become more active and ready to ask questions to enable progress. The use of the mini-white boards can be used to send signals. At any point in the lesson, the teacher can formulate a question which he or she thinks will pose a problem and give students to do on the board and then say "show me." All the boards will go up because this is common practise even if they struggle, but the teacher will be able to check answers to see who really needs help. The teacher is now able to do what the National Entitlement State supports, which is effective teaching and learning with good quality formative assessment whilst making sure to give feedback to students on levels achieved and what to do to move to another level. The big question is, while I am sure that the effective use of mini-whiteboard in Mathematics classes will improve teaching and learning, can it motivate a positive attitude change and can it be used on its own, thus eliminating the use of workbooks.?

Coaching and Mentoring

The implementation of this new strategy adds to the dynamics of a lesson. It also adds to the number of tasks the teacher has to monitor throughout the lesson. One of these is the distribution and collection of equipment at the start of and at the end of lessons. Working with my mentor an Assistant Principal and Line Manager of Mathematics department, we discovered a way of simplifying the distribution and collection of equipment. The classroom consists of three columns. Equipment is placed on the desk of the front table of each column and then passed down to the back by students. At the end of the lesson, the equipment is passed to the front. The numbers of pens are counted by the students sitting at the front tables who were in charge of ensuring that all pens are returned with lids on. As the use of the whiteboards became more and more a part of the normal practice of the lessons, the students were asked to leave pens and boards on table in an organized way. There were also the incidents of students sending inappropriate messages on boards when they were asked to show work, they had these messages on the back of their boards. Working with my coach and mentor we decided that the Teaching Assistant will stand at the back in order to spot students that are doing this. Once the first detention was given and the behaviour was constantly negatively reinforced, this problem was solved.

My mentor thought it was a good idea for me to observe him using the mini-white boards in my lesson so that he could demonstrate how to use the whiteboards effectively. He then requested that I do the following lesson in a similar fashion and asked me to be creative. This form of mentoring is very good because you actually see a demonstration of what you are supposed to do. This however could have had a negative effect if I had tried to copy my mentor. I maintained that I had limitations and that I am in a process of learning. I delivered my demonstration and at the end of the lesson I evaluated my strengths and weaknesses. Also, the fact that he is an Assistant Principal meant that naturally he had more class control because the students tend to be more respectful to a higher hierarchy. I was not deterred by this fact. What I did was to keenly observe his general attitude and mannerism and command of the Mathematical concepts and the fact that he could make questions very quickly out of his head. There was an activity he called "Last man standing." This activity involved giving two students a question. After receiving the question, their answer should be written on the mini-whiteboard as quickly as possible. The student who gives the correct answer first remains standing. The process would continue with two more students until the last man standing who would be the winner. He then gives a reward to the winner.

In observing this, what was amazing, in addition to the fact that the students absolutely loved it, was his ability to provide numerous questions that were relevant to the lesson's objective in quick succession. I thought initially that this persona was a little bit too much for a normal classroom teacher. I started off by preparing questions on paper. Now I am still not as quick as my mentor, but I have made dramatic improvements in this regard. He made reference about it in a departmental meeting.

As stated by Donovan (2005; 39) all professionals should aspire to produce effective teaching and learning within their practice. I thought my mentor was very instrumental in developing my pedagogy to a very high level. Though there is always room for growth, I thought that he inspired in me the ability to take on new challenges without reservations. I am also impressed with the growth of my relationship with my students. The students have now showed more confidence in me as their teacher and they are more confident to perform in the classroom activities because of the improved climate for learning. My mentor was very instrumental in the achievement of this and according to Glover and Law (2002) teacher-student relationships are fundamental to effective learning and teaching

Planning the Professional Learning and Change Activity and carrying out the Plan

The study will adopt a pre-test and a post-test, with three experimental groups (two KS4 and one KS3) and one control group (KS4). At the start of the study, students from all the groups will be asked to grade their interest in Mathematics class and results will be recorded. I will observe and question students to discover their locus of attitude and provide opportunities for class participation to ascertain the locus of class participation. There will be two pre-tests. One pre-test will be done before the introduction of the mini-white board and another at the end of the first lesson, having introduced the mini-white boards. I will refer to this as pre-test because the strategy is not fully implemented, but is only just introduced. The students will be asked to score their interest in the lesson and to talk about their level of participation when compared with the conventional strategy of teaching.

I will ensure that each student has a mini-white board, a new pen and a very good eraser. The students will be introduced to two techniques. The first technique is called "Show Me." This is where the students will be given a question then given a reasonable time to complete the working out on their board and display their answer. The display of this will only be done when the teacher asks them to do so by saying "one, two, three show me". At this time, all the boards should go up. I will then check all boards quickly and then say "ok, thanks, fantastic, put your boards down." The second technique will be done more speedily, where students will answer questions as quickly as possible and put boards up. The first person to put their board up will be given a reward. The student will keep their board up until teacher says "all boards up." This will help to me to detect the students' weaknesses and strengths.

To make the study more successful and valid, I will employ the experience of my mentor who is an Assistant Principal and line manager of Mathematics. He will demonstrate the different skills and techniques and motivate the students to use the whiteboards by providing exciting and friendly competitive activities. The use of rewards will be used to motivate students to perform. The Assistant Principal will set the standards, for example, collecting and distributing equipment. Equipment will be placed at the first table of each column and then passed to the back. The students sitting at the front table will be delegated the responsibility of ensuring that all the equipment are returned at the end of the lessons in an acceptable and desirable way.

Alluding to the fact that high standards are set and the expectations of the groups are very high, I will ensure that these standards are kept and will give regular progress report to my mentor and ask for ideas or suggestions where necessary.

Plan Executed

Using the Mini-White Board, the students were given their boards and ten quick questions were done. These questions were related to previous learning and also intended to develop pre-requisite knowledge. The first question was below the level of all the students. This got the desired result, which was full class participation, providing and setting the tone for the lesson. A classroom filled with praises, the words fantastic, well done and absolutely brilliant were some of the words and phrases that were used. In some instances students were given tangible rewards. The levels of questions were then gradually increased. While full class participation was encouraged, the speed of the response was decreased.

The students were given allotted time according to the level of difficulty of the questions. Differentiation was also done with respect to time and the level of students. Some students were given more time than others. The use of the interactive board was used to display and demonstrate concepts to boost knowledge and understanding of pre-requisite skills. Discussions were also done to encourage full class participation and enhance general understanding of concept and also to clear up misconceptions. Some students were given kinaesthetic material to help them with the concept. Having gone through a number of examples, the students were given three questions to do on mini-white boards. When students were ready, they were introduced to the topic. Again interactive boards, discussions, examples and kinaesthetic materials were used to develop concept. The students were then asked to do questions on mini-white boards then display answer when asked to do so. I checked to see when students were comfortable to work on their own, at which time they were given questions to do and record in their workbook. As the level increased, I made general checks by asking students to do questions on white boards and displaying it. Depending on the results produced I got whole class attention and re-explained or gave individual assistance.

A vital element to a lesson is to have the students leaving the room with the feeling that they have achieved. To facilitate this important concept I used mini-white boards to do more 'Show me' activities. Again I gave questions below the students' level and then increased the level of the questions gradually. Students received lots of praise as they were now working above their level. At end of the lesson they knew the level they reached in the topic. This was followed up in following lesson.

Presenting and Analysing Results

Consequent to my experiment, all the classes improved in general behaviour and attitude towards mathematics. There was however variations in levels of improvements achieved. What was surprising is that group D, my control group did show improvements in general behaviour and attitude. I had to however conclude that because there were several factors that attributed to this change, such as my general attitude, my improved pedagogy, different students, time of lessons and the class they had before my class, the control group was not very significant and relevant in comparing and contrasting the outcome of implementing the mini-white board as opposed to not using them.

Groups A, B and C were very much appreciative of the new initiative and were excited about shifting from the contemporary and monotonous use of the workbook. There was to some extent a notion that the use of another initiative might have brought this change. This gave the impression that the change did not necessarily come about because of the mini-white boards. Groups A and B had a fluctuating 2-3% of students who were not fully fascinated and encouraged by the importance of mini-white boards and hence displayed poor attitude in some of the lessons. The participation and the general ethos that was created mainly by the majority of the students, who were cognisant of the objective of the new strategy, however, did help to influence a positive change in their attitude. I am not convinced at this point that they have made that progress.

Group C was far more receptive to the use of the mini-white board than the other groups and they displayed very good use of them. They were keen to compete against each other. In most of the lessons they requested boys against girls competitions. The boys who generally struggled in the lessons were motivated to perform and did use the principles explained to ask for help.

Group D did show a level of growth in terms of their enthusiasm towards mathematics lessons. This, when compared to the other groups were however less than the other groups who were introduced to the mini-white boards. I am aware of the fact that my enthusiasm and pedagogy was improved leaving me to wonder if this has made an impacted on the students. In this group however, students who struggled still tend to shy away from asking for help. This was a significant difference with the use of the mini-white boards as there were easy ways of showing this without been subjected to class ridicule. The students who struggled were only picked up when I walked around and checked in addition to when peer assessment was done.

Consequently the students' level of attainment increased. This was evident in the assessment done at the end of every chapter called the Chapter Review. Each text book used has its own chapter review which is designed to test students' level of attainment in each chapter. It is mandatory that each teacher carry out these tests and outline success criteria to students. After marking the test students were given a sticker showing "on target,""above target" or "below target" depending on the number of success criteria met. It was evident that the number of student getting above target in group A increased from 10 to 15 and the number of student getting on target decreased from 15 to 13. Also the number of students who were getting below target decreased from 5 to 2. There was a similar trend in group B and C however, in group C the level of students getting above target rose from 9 to 18.

The group that was the control group did show a level of improvement in attainment with regards to chapter review. There was an increase in above target from 11 to 14 and a decrease in the number of below target from 6 to 3. It must be noted that having done five chapter reviews there was a consistently growing trend in group A, B, and C. The changes in group D did show some level of fluctuation. I am still not able to conclude that these results are entirely based on the introduction of the effective use of the mini-white board. I could however conclude that the level of attitude and participation in mathematics was increased as a result of the new strategy of using the use of the mini-white boards. I have also improved my pedagogy and have such my lesson presentations improved.

Sharing Learning, Influencing Practice and Evaluating Learning

I was given the opportunity by my HOD, organised by my mentor, to present findings in a Mathematics department meeting. I demonstrated the use of the mini-white boards to the department outlining some of the basic skills used and also the rationale for these skills. The fact that the students could show or reveal that they needed help without actually saying it was really well received by all. The teachers were extremely happy to try the mini-whiteboards in their lesson as they were facing similar challenges with the students not wanting to ask for help because they feared class ridicule, some were just too shy and that students complained about writing in books all the time. Some even complained that the lessons were too boring. Most of the teachers, while adamant that this was a good practice and that they would definitely try it, were still not happy about the number of equipment that they would have to distribute and collect at the start and end of lessons and that there would be the problem of students taking away the pens. I was however quick to assure teachers that there is an easy way to alleviate these problems. I told them that at the end of the lessons simply ask the students to put the lids on pens and leave the pens and mini-whiteboards on tables in an orderly way. This can be then used with the following class. Students should leave the room table by table and they only leave until their table is checked and the teacher is satisfied.

I showed the teachers my students' workbooks and they were impressed at the level of students who were now receiving "above target" ratings and also the fact that some students who usually gave trouble in other lessons were now meeting targets and some although not meeting the desired targets were showing a level of improvement. The fact that students only record in their books when they are absolutely sure that working out and answer is correct was also an amazing discovery. This is due to the fact that my students' books were regularly marked and were showing correct answers with beautiful ticks. I explained that the students took more pride writing in books when they are absolutely sure that what they are writing is correct hence the quality of the presentation in their books.

Evaluating My Learning

At the start of the project I was very excited but in some ways not exactly sure of how the students would respond. This limited my level of confidence. My mentor was very instrumental in getting me off to a very good start. He came and demonstrated the skills perfectly well and set a very high standard for me to maintain. This was very good for me because I was just a normal classroom teacher trying to emulate an Assistant Principal. I however maintained that I am a good teacher and that I was going to be myself. I was cognisant of the fact that all good teachers make mistakes. All good teachers start off with a number of weaknesses but with practice and experience gained over time, they convert the weaknesses into professional strengths. Distributing and collecting the whiteboards and pens along with workbooks and sometimes other kinaesthetic equipment every lesson was a very big task. This was however eliminated once the discovery and implementation of the whiteboards and pens staying on the table to be used in following lessons was implemented.

Getting the students to use the mini-white boards correctly was very easy, as mentioned before, this was demonstrated by my mentor. The majority of students were excited with the implementation of the new strategy and that they were able to make a shift from the conventional monotonous method. While the majority of students adopted the new strategy and became functionalists and ambassadors for the strategy, there were also the "againsters." These were the undecided few who were not cognisant of the real rationale for the implementation of the use of the mini-white boards and some who could not care less. Consequently, there were a few issues with students passing undesirable messages to other students on the back of their whiteboards. Having reported and discussed this with my mentor, we decided that the learning support should stand at the back when students were showing their answers. A few detentions were issued and this problem was solved.

The infectious enthusiasm displayed by the majority of students and myself soon took over the classes. The lessons were filled with a glow of excitement and hence the students were willing to perform. The fact that we were able to do diagnostic testing very efficiently was a huge success. In addition, there was the opportunity to carry out formative assessment during the lessons. This helped the teacher to address students' needs individually as this was easily identified by using the mini-white board. Students who before were reluctant to write in their books were now willing to write in their books after their work was checked on the mini-white boards and found to be correct. Students were happy that most or all in some cases, that the work that were recorded in their books were correct. Their books became a vital and good source of reference.

I was very happy with the success so far. What I wanted to try in future was to have students working in groups using the mini-white boards and to try to develop a team bonding. Students were asked to share and decide answers amongst group members before displaying boards. This enhanced the use of peer discussion, peer assessment and peer evaluation. In addition to that, another of my aim was to have students leading some of the sessions. Students would make and present power point presentations and get feedback from students by asking them prepared questions. Students would respond by using their mini-white boards. Getting students to this level would pose some level of challenge as some of the students did not have a very high level of self-confidence. Getting a selective group to perform the task two or three times would definitely develop group leaders who would be placed in separate groups to motivate and lead others.

As a result of the school being changed to an Academy, the theme is based on success culture. The overall management is keen to support any change that will develop students' confidence, performance, general attitude, general behaviour and hence academic performance.

References
Ackroyd, J (2006) Research Methodologies for Drama Education
Trentham Books LTD
734 London Road.

Leading Educational change through Motivation and Mentoring

Motivation and mentoring are two vital roles of leaders in education. Wallace and Gravells (2007) said that if we think about leaders who have connected with us in any way that was motivating and energising, part of their influence will probably have stemmed from their own enthusiasm for what they were doing and what they were trying to achieve. Motivating staff to perform is of vital importance if they are going to be energized to give the best they can in order to obtain maximum performance from their students. According to Pintrich and Scunk (1996) students are motivated by learning something useful or important, by feeling of progress, by performing well, and, for some students, by performing better than others. It is always better to motivate staff by using positive comments even when things are not going as planned than to use only negative comments. This will help to empower and to impress upon staff that their effort is valued although the desired result was not obtain but they will be motivated to try again until success is achieved. When this success is achieved the staff will feel good about themselves and hence will go on to achieve even more. Mentoring is very important and in some cases work together with motivation. According to Waid, Bossons and Gover (2004) mentoring is a mutual learning partnership in which individuals assist each other with personal and career development through coaching, role modelling, counselling, sharing knowledge and providing emotional support. An efficient and effective way of leading a change is by demonstrating or modelling the concept. By mentoring other staff the opportunity is created for mentor to demonstrate activities and to model expected attitudes and management skills. Ward, Bossons and Gover (2004) also stated that behind every successful person, there is one elementary truth: somewhere, someone cared about their growth and development. Consequently I will be studying motivation and reflect on the impact of my motivational strategies on other staff. I will also study mentoring to gain a better understanding of this management role and also reflect on the impact of my mentorship provided to other staff in my department.

Motivation can be categorised in two ways, intrinsic and extrinsic. Intrinsic motivation is when the individual is inspired from within to perform a given task. The individual is driven by internal force or internal motives. Conversely external motivation is when the individual or the practitioner is motivated by external forces. There are debates as to which type of motivation really causes the individual to perform at maximum potential. If someone is intrinsically motivated to perform one could argue that this person will perform to maximum for a longer period even when the circumstances or task become challenging. The extrinsically motivated person will always need that proverbial dangling of carrot in front their eyes. There is a strong possibility that they will not perform at maximum when there is no carrot and the task become tedious. The extent to which these two types of motivation vary can best be ascertained through observing the end results of task given to perform by individuals.

Motivating and Mentoring Staff to improve Classroom Management.

Class room Management is of paramount importance for effective learning and teaching. This is a complex and dynamic concept but when mastered will provide very good benefits. Classroom can be categorised in two groups the physical and the psycho-social hence classroom management will be looked at in terms of managing the physical resources and the psycho-social environment. I am very conscious that students learn mostly from what they see. Busher and Harris (2006) postulated that effective learning and teaching does not occur by accident. It is usually the product of an effective classroom situation created by a skilful teacher. I am conscious that students learn through the hidden curriculum. With these concepts in mind consequently, I ensure that my classroom is properly organised and that all books and equipment are stored in an obvious systematic order. I ensure that my classroom has the necessary lighting and that the window blinds are in place for protection from the rays of the sun which can prevent students' from seeing the interactive board properly. I also ensure that my classroom has effective heating supply for winter seasons.

Seating plans are in place for groups that normally causes disruption. All equipment is packed away and classroom is properly cleared and cleaned before the class is allowed to enter or leave the room. The students tend to appreciate the classroom when it is very clean and tidy; they are also intrinsically motivated to leave it in a clean an orderly manner as well. I am also aware of secondary learning therefore I carefully display educational facts and motivational charts in my classroom. The educational facts are organised in terms of the different strands in the mathematics curriculum. Students' works are checked and some are also displayed in the respective strand as well. My classroom consists of twenty computers. It is very frustrating for students when they are asked to work on the computers and they sat behind a computer only to realize that they are unable to log on or the mouse is not working. As a result of this, I check the computers every evening and report as quickly as possible any problems or challenges noticed. If the technicians are not able to fix it before the start of the lesson, I usually put a note pad on the computer to say that it is out of use. This tends to alleviate the frustration.

Creating a good physical environment is very important with respect to classroom management but is it more important than maintaining a good positive psycho-social environment or, are they as equally important? Whatever the answer is both are vital to create a classroom conducive to learning and teaching. This cannot be taken lightly and as such I have placed great emphasis on continued studies and learning to inform my planning in this regard. Students must feel safe to perform and not only to perform but to perform at their best. I ensure that I exercise a level of consistency and fairness in all my lessons. As Mortimore (1993) state that effective teachers bind together skills and knowledge through the use of their imagination I used the school policies to enhance creativity and sensitivity in order to stimulate, support and encourage learning using means as high expectation and modelling behaviour. Consequently I maintain a level of consistency when dealing with all behavioural issues and maintain a fair but strict approach to dealing with undesirable behaviour.

Students are very keen on noticing and been out spoken about inconsistency. This is what I have learned through experience. Now I am more aware of the importance of consistency therefore, this has become a part of my pedagogy practice. Most, if not all students like to work in a controlled environment, even the students who tends to disrupt lessons. When these students continually push for boundaries and they eventually find their boundary with a teacher they will stop at that boundary and of course will try to push again sometimes later. Should students challenge school policy? Should more mature and able student be a part of school making policies? These seem to be very interesting questions. However because I maintain my consistency with school policy regardless of challenge they soon find out that undesired behaviour will be punished. This helped to create an effective climate for learning and teaching within the classroom. I know my students individually. I know their mode of learning therefore I prepare my lesson to meet their needs. All students are catered for. I generally start my lesson using the concept of the J curve where students are given task below their level to boost their confidence and raise their concept of self as mathematicians and then gradually take them to maximum possible progressive level.

To what extent is high expectation of students and praise impact on their learning? As soon as my students enter my classroom they are immersed into a "pool" of praise and high expectations. Constant praise is given for all areas of work even if answer is incorrect. Students are praised for effort and motivated to try again. I motivate my students by using APP. After each assessment, the students are told the level they have achieved and sometimes they are told the level of questions that they will be working on before they start. I always tell my students that I expect them to be the best mathematicians in the school. After they finish their task I always emphasize the point that if they are going to be the best mathematician in the school they need to move to another level. They are then motivated to perform at their highest level. Achievements are praised and celebrated in a number of ways including awarding certificate to students of the month. This motivates students to want to perform better each day.

I also improve the psycho-social environment of my classroom by giving students roles and responsibilities. Do these roles really impact on the psycho-social environment or do the names of the roles enhance this effect? These roles are carefully named to motivate them to feel a sense of achieving and valued. One such role is Environmental Manager, who is in charge of making sure that all equipment are returned and packed away neatly, and there are no litter left on the floor. The students in charge of these roles are changed monthly as this becomes a privilege and not a right. The students have to work towards achieving this or these roles. Students look forward to be called Environmental Manager or Group Motivator.

I motivate other staff to use some of my effective practise by discussion in departmental meetings and general staff meeting. I have also encouraged other staff within my department to visit my lesson at any time they pleased and also to do arranged full lesson observation. I have also observed other teacher lessons and gave them credit for their good practise and also ask them for permission to use some of their practises in my lessons. I generally evaluate these practises and try to improve on them. I offer mentoring to new staff in my department. To facilitate this I encourage them to do full lesson observation and also to team teach with me. Is team teaching a good an effective practise to improve other teachers' pedagogy skills or does it damage their confidence? While there will always be the questions of what are the students thinking about the teacher of the class? If team teaching is done properly it does have more positive impact on all involve.

Motivating Staff to use AVK.

Marris (1993) argues there is a major difference between voluntary and imposed change and that peoples responses to all change is to feel loss, anxiety and struggle. Accepting these responses as a natural and necessary part of the change process is important for the subject leader. Teachers who are used to the conventional chalk and talk style of delivering their lessons to students, where they intend to pour into 'empty mugs', do find it difficult to accept the concept of AVK. Can you be an effective teacher if you are not aware of your students' mode of learning? It was suggested about a year ago by an Assistant Principal that all teachers should provide the mode of learning of all the students in their lesson. This survey was done by most of the teachers. Therefore there is a data base containing the students learning mode. While some teachers will argue that not all mathematics lessons are possible to teach using all the three modes, some are of the opinion that if we are conscious of the students learning mode and an effort is been made to meet this need then learning and teaching will become more effective. I rely heavily on this vital information to form the basis of my planning and delivery of my lessons. I motivate other teachers to do the same by showing them the results of the students and the level of work they were able to achieve by working within their learning mode.

According to Bloom's Taxonomy, lesson objective should foster three domains. The Cognitive Domain which is based on the knowledge learnt, the Psycho-motive which is based on the activities and practical skills done and finally the Affective Domain which is the feeling. How much did the students appreciated the task, is it relevant to everyday life, did the students learn to work together and to appreciate others opinion. These domains along with fostering good use of AVK will help students to become more active learners and will develop them into more rounded individuals who will eventually play an integral role in society. Mathematics should be taught for life not just for the sake of passing GCSE. It is a given that using AVK stimulate the interest of the students and also it helps to gain full class participation. Full class participation does alleviate and eliminate undesirable behaviour. If this is however a proven fact, then why is it that teachers still have a fair amount of reluctance to engage in the sort of planning and preparation that will make this learning and teaching possible and constant?

Moon (2005) states that the influence of a teacher in encouraging a learner to engage in a material is a matter of how the learner perceives the teacher and their teaching as well as more objective qualities of the teaching such as organization of the material clarity and enthusiasm. Good teaching can facilitate a deep approach. I am intrinsically motivated to use AVK in my lesson planning and hence in my lesson. The contagious and infectious enthusiasm and zeal that I possess motivates other teacher in my department to use AVK. I also share my lesson plans with other teachers and during administrative period I discuss with teachers in my department the importance and demonstrate the effective use of AVK. Teachers are now motivated to use AVK as well because they realize that it helps to promote full class participation and that it is a recommended tool to incorporate all the domain stated by Bloom's Taxonomy and also that it stimulates the interest of the students and helps to develop their functional skills. It is the development of these functional skills that will enable students to play an integral role in society. According to Parson, Education is the transmission of society's norms and values. Some teachers are now using AVK even though they still argue that before these concepts were in place students used to perform better than they are performing now. They still believe that students should just 'get on with it' no matter the style or method been used.

Most teachers are knowledgeable of their subject and also are confident about their teaching qualities. They will therefore proudly boast that they are good teachers. While this is good, one must ask several questions after a lesson. What have the students learnt? Have I met my learning objectives? This process of evaluating ones teaching with respect to what the students have learnt is the all Hallmark of good teaching and learning. The good teacher will therefore plan for Assessment of Learning.

Is there a specific time or place for Assessment for learning during a lesson? This is still subject to debate. What is important though is that it is done and be carried out effectively. The lesson has not been taught until the students have learnt. Assessment for learning can be done at the start of a lesson and is called Diagnostic Testing or during the lesson which is called Formative Testing where feedback is given and instructions as to how to make progress or also at the end of the lesson which is used to inform planning for future lesson. By doing an AFL in every lesson teacher and students are able to identify students' individual weaknesses and strengths. This helps both parties to work out strategies to foster growth and progress. During my course to gain Qualify Teacher Status (QTS) I was trained by my course leader and also my school mentor to effectively use AFL. I have also gone to many CPD sessions to develop my skills in using AFL. I have several lesson observations gaining excellent and good for the use of AFL.

Moon (2005) stated that a SWOT analysis is a commonly used tool that facilitates intense thinking or studying about an issue or event. It involves the separate noting of issues under the four words that make up the acronym; Strengths, Weaknesses, Opportunities and Threats. These words do play a part in learning and teaching exercise and should be evaluated both from the teacher and the students' perspective. I have asked a teacher in my department in a jokingly way "What lesson have you just taught?" and the teacher answered confidently, "Using Pythagoras' Theorem to find missing side." When I asked her "What have the students learnt?" her confidence decreased down then she replied, "I suppose that they have learnt to use Pythagoras theorem to find missing side." When I asked "how do you know that the students have learnt this?" she then realised that I was asking her if she had done an Assessment for Learning. Assessment for Learning is not an entirely new concept to teaching but it can be forgotten or it can be taken lightly by some teachers if they don't see the real importance.

As a result, I have shared my folder with staff in my department who were at that time doing their QTS course. I have influenced them to use AFL by showing them that this is an important aspect of a lesson and also that this is a key factor that any assessor will look for. These teachers are now making use of AFL and also they have made massive progress in their pedagogy skills which they have shared in Mathematics Department Meetings. Assessment for learning is a must do in every lesson. Can a lesson be considered complete without the teacher finding out what the students have learnt? Can strengths and weaknesses be evaluated without Assessment for learning?

Throughout a student's academic sojourn, target setting is of paramount importance and does play a vital role in tracking students' progress. There is a tracking system in place in my department. This is made available to all staff members. I am cognisant of the fact that tracking students' progress is not just another piece of statistical data for principals and senior management but it is a useful tool to inform planning. Tracking system does provide the actual level of each student and their target for the end of term and for they end of year. I do motivate teachers in my department to use these statistical data to guide their planning. I have met with teachers on individual and group basis to critically analyse this statistical data and also have tried to improve the recording of the data. All the teachers are now aware of their students target and also they are aware of where they are and how to improve their target. I have also encouraged teachers in my department to request from the HOD opportunities to go on courses to facilitate further development and training in assessing students' progress and raising attainments.

Teachers are now motivated to use this statistical data to guide and inform their planning and as a result their teaching has become more purposeful and students are now more responsive as they are able to see that they are making progress. Teachers are also motivated to make use of levelling in their tasks where students are able to see the level of task they are working on. After the assessments, students are usually praised by informing them that they have achieved for example a level five, and that they can make progress to level six. The feeling of growth and making progress do motivate students and when students are motivated this in turn will motivate teachers as well. Every teacher has a perception of themselves as a teacher, likewise every students has a perception of themselves as a mathematician. This perception of self is what motivates both parties to perform. Fortunately this perception of self can be consciously or unconsciously improved. Teachers can improve their perception of themselves by making a concerted effort to increase their knowledge and improve their pedagogy skills. I have motivated teachers in my department to measure the perception that they have of themselves as teacher and by doing this, hey have raised their level of perception. Students when realizing that they are attaining their target and are also working above target, though not fully aware of the ideology the perception of self will unconsciously raise their perception of self as mathematician. The more this is raised the more students will be motivated to perform.

Understanding and using statistical data to guide planning is vital the attainment of this important aspect for both teachers and students. What are the barriers to learning and teaching? According to Piaget and his Theory of Assimilation and accommodation, if a child holds the perception of a cow as something looking like a star, but in essence a cow is shaped like the moon, the teacher is faced with the problem of getting the child to accommodate and assimilate the new concept. Far too often students will respond to teaching by saying I don't get it. I have motivated and inspired teachers within my department to look at Jean Piaget's theory to help them to understand what the students are experiencing. After understanding this concept, they were faced with the problem of solving it. I clearly outlined to them that every student has a scheme of thoughts and ideas in their brain about mathematical concepts. They will tend to hold onto this as their personal belonging so it is therefore imperative that teachers try to draw knowledge from their students and then critically analyse and synthesise it to create the actual fact.

Another important tool in teaching that I have also motivated teachers to use is Ausubel Organiser. This is where teachers give the students' time to research the concept before trying to teach it. In my department a website called My Maths is widely used and some teachers give their students software called Maths Watch. I have asked my HOD to make this available to all the students. This Maths Watch software is an audio-visual software with all the topics on it. Students are able to listen and watch any topic they wish to. By using the principle of Ausubel Organiser I have motivated teachers to ask their students to prepare before lesson. In a case where the teacher will teach Rationalising Surds in their next lesson, the students are told before the class to use My Maths and or Maths Watch to research all they can about rationalising surds. Teachers are also motivated to reward students who show that they have done intense research. What this does is to create the right concept in the students' scheme what surds are. They are more able to accommodate and assimilate this new concept because they are prepared to do so and in this case rather than hearing "don't get it," teachers will hear "I knew that." An "I knew that" response from a student is the hallmark of good teaching as the students will feel that this is coming from them and not just the teacher. They will want to go and research more.

I have also motivated teachers to use prompting and fading. This is where if the teacher is looking for an answer, rather than telling the students, the students are prompted to give the answer. If for example the answer is acute, rather than telling the students that the answer is acute, a good teacher will write the letter A then C then U then T and by this time at least one student will say acute. This is an opportunity to give praise and must be taken. A good teacher will say fantastic, well done, give her a round of applause etc. This help to put the students at the forefront of their learning and they will leave the class with that feeling of achieving and thus their perception of self as mathematician will grow.

Understanding and Evaluating Policy

Bushers and Harris (2000) stated that the first barriers to change are the lack of access to information about the change itself. For many teachers change is simply imposed from above or externally generated. The students tend to feel the same way as well. Should teachers and students play more active role in creating school policies? Teachers who understand and use school policy are far better able to develop good climate for learning. But do all teachers know, understand and use the policies? I have been asked by other teachers to keep disruptive students in my class and most of the times the students will say that the teacher doesn't like them or the teacher is picking on them. Though I do not hold it in my mind, this is always the case I was concerned about. The fact that students are able to make these assumptions about other teachers, maybe they say the same things about me. It became imperative for me to discover something that would totally or at least try to eradicate the students' view. The idea of consistency was brought to mind. I become more aware of this concept and as such led to the fact that the easiest way to be consistent is to know and understand the school policies and to use them at all times. I have now posted the school behaviour policy in my classroom and have then motivated other teachers to do the same. This is used as a visual for disruptive students. They are made to refer to the policy and they now become aware that the decision I am taking is not based on by own judgement but it is the school's policy. They are now aware of the consequences that will follow the different forms of undesirable behaviour. By using the policy at all times with all students are not in a position to say that I am picking on them or at worst I don't like them. I have motivated other teachers in my department to copy and display a copy of the policy in their classroom and to make reference to it at all time when dealing with disruptive students.

It is always important to make a positive comment before disciplining a student. This will help to erase the negative thought from their minds that the teacher is picking on them or don't like them. By telling the student that he has been excellent last lesson or he has started out very well today or he shows good potential in maths, this will help to minimise any danger. If poor behaviour persists, then the teacher will then refer the student to Behaviour Policy and then take action. Though this does not always prevent students from making assumptions, it does reduce the extent to which any damage is done by getting other students to believe that the teacher does not like them. The other students in the class will also see that the teacher is been consistent with is only applying the school policy.

Can every child learn mathematics or can every child make good progress in mathematics? Pintrich and Schunk (1996) state that students who feel self-confident about learning and performing well in school seek challenges, expand effort to learn new material, and persist at difficult task. The questions must that must be asked is "Are we as teachers providing a classroom climate, activities and opportunities to develop the confidence of our students?" All students are important and as such teachers must take the responsibility of ensuring that all students in their classroom are given the opportunity to learn. It is a given that some students learn at a faster rate than some and also that the level of ability in the class varies. This fact led to the point that care must be taken to facilitate inclusion where all students are catered for and intervention strategies are put in place to facilitate the development of all students. I have motivated teachers in my department to share their lesson plans with teaching assistant and also when necessary to plan with their teaching assistant for specific students who need additional support. The idea of preparing differentiated work was also explored and this has had a great impact on students' participation in class.

As differentiation is done by levelling, students aspire to work to improve their level and support is made available to help them to do so. There are also clear directions as to how to make progress. Students are not given multiple tasks at the same level. As soon as the teacher identifies that the students have mastered a level, the teacher provide the opportunity for students to make progress. I have helped and motivated teachers in my department to move away from this conventional method of teaching, for example where students spend an entire lesson adding fractions with the same denominator for the entire lesson. Teachers are now motivated to move on to examples with different denominators and then on to mixed fractions and also to move on to multiplying and dividing fractions with some students who are ready to progress. In essence, the lessons are not geared towards a certain level but a range of levels. For example, a good teacher will inform their class that today they will move from level 3a to level 5a and some students depending on their work rate will move to level 6c or above. The tasks that are provided for the students are levelled, therefore students are able to see what they must do to get to the next level. Each level of attainment is met with some form of reward. Praises are most often used and in some instances tangible items are given. What effect does praises have on students' performance and holistic development?

This is now a departmental policy and teachers are highly motivated to use this concept in all their lessons. Most teachers have now displayed charts in their class showing different questions and their level in all the strands. Students are able to see that the teachers really think about helping them to make progress. Also the text books that are now used in the department have the level of the questions written beside them so students are able to see what level of question they are working at.

I could not lave my sojourn as a teacher without sharing with you some work that I did on behaviour. I know that these studies are important to you because we all have to relate and deal with people. A king is born.

TITLE: THE USE OF MODIFICATION STRATEGIES TO IMPROVE LEARNER BEHAVIOUR WITHIN A SECONDARY SCHOOL

Aim: Identify methods of improving learner behaviour

Objectives:

1. Identify what is poor behaviour
2. Evaluate the reasons for poor learner behaviour
3. Critique behaviour modification strategies for use within a classroom
4. Make recommendation for the school

Methods: Desk Research, Literature Review and Case Study.

Approximately 8000 words.

On a daily basis, many teachers deal with disruptions arising from students' inappropriate behaviours. Such behaviours may include talking out of turn, not following instructions, and not interacting properly with peers (Corrie, 1997). Such disruptive classroom behaviours significantly impact teachers' capacity to maintain a productive and orderly learning environment and has been repeatedly found to be a major factor contributing to teacher stress, discontent, and burn-out (Chazan, et al., 1994; Ellis & Magee, 1999; Hawe, Tuck, Manthei, Moore, 2000; Merrett&Wheldall, 1993; Rutherford &DiGangi, 1991; Sterling-Turner, Robinson)

According to Wearmouth, Richmond, Glyn (2004) students who are non-compliant or display anti-social behaviours are an ongoing concern for school staff and parents throughout the world. There are several diagnostic categories and terms describing these students including: Children with Emotional and Behaviour Difficulties (EBD), Conduct Disordered (CD) (Fox & Stinnnett, Delinquent, Emotionally handicapped (EH), Oppositional Defiant Disorder (ODD), Severely Emotional / Behaviourally Disordered, Severely Emotionally Disturbed SSED) Socially Maladjusted, Troubled and troubling students as well as others descriptors including : Aggressive, Disruptive and Distractible, Maladjusted, and Severely

Disruptive. These are what we could consider as a sum total of the different types of behaviours patterns displayed by pupils across the schools in the UK and in the rest of the world in at large.

Many teachers find the management of disruptive behaviour very aversive and stressful. In extreme situations such behaviours can jeopardise not only the smooth functioning of classroom, interfering with the process of teaching and learning, but also can threaten the safety of self and others. Further, recurrent inappropriate classroom behaviour has been shown to be predictive of present and future academic under-achievement for the students involved (Malecki & Elliot, 2002; Wentel, 1993).

Researchers have identified that persistent disruptive behaviour may interfere not only with the task of academic learning, but importantly also with the development of social skills, depriving students of social support from their peers. The absence of social skills has been correlated with students' loneliness (Cassidy &Asher 1992). Children with negative and destructive interactive patterns often become catalysts for conflict with peers (Broadhead, 1998), which in turn may result in peer rejection and social isolation. When students are rejected by their peers they have very little sense of belonging. This can lead to students being withdrawn from participation in class activities. If this is identified early the teacher can organise the classroom by using group work to foster development of this social attribute. It is important to make sure that students are motivated and given numerous of social rewards as soon they display an acceptable behaviour.

There is clear evidence that conduct problems are associated with negative long-term outcomes for the students involved, including lowered rates of successful school-completion, increased unemployment, and a higher risk of incarceration (Bear, 1999: Blechman, 1996: Chazan, et al., 1994: Little &Hudson, 1998; Tobin &Sugai, 1999) with associated costs to society. In addition, recurrent disruptive and antisocial classroom behaviour has also been shown to be a problem for other students compromising their participation in academic and social learning opportunities, diverting teacher attention from academic instruction, or simply through the general disruption caused (Kern, Childs, Dunlap, Clarke, & Falk, 1994; Kern, Delaney, Clarke, Dunlap, & Childs, 2001; Sterling-Turner et al., 2001). In extreme cases class peers can also be put at risk of personal harm or injury. In the case of teaching a new concept in mathematics where a number of skills are involved, it is important that teachers make sure that the students have the necessary prerequisite knowledge. This can sometimes lead to the fact that the time to explain the concept may be longer than normal. Students have to be entirely focused if this concept is to be taught properly. If the teacher has to stop at different intervals to address behaviour concerns, then this will cause students to lose sight of the concept and teacher has to start all over again. This can lead to frustration to pupils who genuinely want to get on with learning.

Student Behaviour and Culturalism:

According to Bruner (1996) the cultural context in which a child is reared shapes his / her thinking. Meaning-making is situated in a cultural context as well as in the prior conceptions that learners bring with them into new situations as a result of previous learning in other contexts. New learning is a product of the interplay between them. Bruner raised a number of issues relevant to be considered about student behaviour:

- Where learning is assumed to occur through engagement in society, pedagogy needs to be interactive and inter-subjective to take account of individual meaning-making and allow for the production of shared task outcomes.

- Educational policies and practices need to take account of the fact that schools exist in societies where issues of power, status and rewards are very influential.
- Schooling plays a critical part in shaping a student's sense of 'self', that is in his/her belief in his/her ability, responsibility and skill in initiating and completing actions and task.
- Failing to support the development of students understanding and ability to act in a cultural context risks marginalising and alienating young people and rendering them incompetent, with the consequent threat to the stability of society as a whole.

The way in which schools mediate success and failure are crucial to the development of a sense personal agency. School is an integral part of the culture, not simply a way of preparing for entry. Teachers should therefore reflect continuously on the impact of school processes and practices on young people's sense of agency and ability. As Bruner (1996) notes, one of the prime responsibilities of schools is to support the construction of a student's sense of self through an acknowledgement of agency and development of self esteem. Within an institution, both educators and students are defined by that institution's social practices. Participation in a community is transformative both to participants and to the group (Davies, 2004).

Biological/ Medical explanation of behaviour

Difficult behaviour, from a medical perspective, is the result of an underlying condition or disease which an individual has and which requires treatment. In some cases this may involve the use of medicine, which, in the context of schools, has obvious ethical considerations. Explanations involve a process of diagnosis based on the symptoms to identify the existence of an underlying condition or illness and then intervention or treatment to provide a cure. However, because behaviour is defined within the context of a social grouping, establishing the existence of a condition or disease of difficult behaviour or emotional disorder is fraught with problems. Among the explanations of behaviour experienced as challenging to teachers and often to parents also is the notion of attention deficit/ hyperactivity disorder (AD/HD), described by Norwich et al. (2002):

AD/HD is a medical diagnosis of the American Psychiatric Association. It is characterised by chronic and pervasive (to home and school) problems of inattention, impulsiveness, and or excessive motor activity which have seriously debilitating effects on individuals' social, emotional and educational development, and are sometimes disruptive to the home and or school environment. Between two and five percent of British school children are believed to experience this condition (BP's, 1997). The coming of this diagnosis has revived traditional conflicts between medical and educational perspectives on EBD, which affect the way in which practitioners approach problems surrounding childhood attention and activity problems . . . (Norwich Cooper and Maras, 2002, p. 182)

The defining features of AD/HD are behaviour which appears inattentive, impulsive and overactive to an extent that is unwarranted for their developmental age and is a significant hindrance to their social and educational success' (BPS, 1996, p. 13). In Britain and Europe, unlike the USA, the tradition has been' to use the diagnostic systems of the International Classification of Diseases (ICD) published by the World Health Organization' and to assume a 'hyperkinetic disorder'. There is a strict requirement for 'pervasiveness and persistence' which means that behaviour seen largely in one context only does not constitute grounds for a diagnosis. One major explanation of behaviour that relates very closely to a medical model of disability is Autism.

Autism and its characteristics

All people with autism have impairments in social interaction, social communication and imagination. This is referred to as the triad of impairments. People with social interaction impairment tend to have difficulty with social relationships, for example appearing aloof and indifferent to other people. People with social communication impairment tend to have difficulty with verbal and non-verbal communication, for example, not really understanding the meaning of gestures, facial expressions or tone of voice. Finally people with imagination impairment have difficulty in the development of play and imagination, for example having a limited range of imagination activities, possibly copied and pursued rigidly and repetitively.

Historical and Cultural Roots of Behaviour

The subject of behaviour is both long in historical connections and multi-disciplinary in nature. The nature of behaviour and reactions also tends to fluctuate along a wide continuum of tolerance. At one end is the libertarian bias that seems to stand against any suggestion of restriction individual freedom of choice, an almost total 'rights zone' that is free of any balancing responsibilities. At the other end is the early

Spartan ethic, that individuals should be trained in the services of the collective good, which in this case was the needs of a military society, 'responsibility writ large' with little room for individual rights. Somewhere in between come the arguments that individual expressions must not be stifled nor allowed to roam free and uncontrolled—rather, human behaviour has to be shaped until its holder reaches some position of accepting self-discipline and the equilibrium of personal rights balanced with personal responsibilities.

Until recent decades, the conceptualisation of behaviour and behaviour difficulties has been focused largely on the individual and the individual perspective. Questions such as why does she behave like that? or why can't he control this behaviour? Have been centre stage. Answering them has been approached either by viewing behaviour as pathology, that is, a disorder stemming from early experiences trapped in the unconscious or subconscious mind, or as caused by physical factors, or by focusing on how exhibited behaviour has been learned and how it may need to be ameliorated and restricted. The focus on abnormal behaviour has led to what has come to be known as the Medical Model of human functioning. The notion of disorder has resulted in whole range therapies for treating behaviour that is troublesome for the individual or the community.

The concept of disorders is at the extreme end of the troublesome spectrum, and the idea of psychosomatic conditions is at the milder end. Though much earlier somatic therapy has been abandoned, as the power of the medical model has lessened under the influence of new insights and new approaches, many perceived behavioural abnormalities or behavioural difficulties are still treated using chemotherapy, electrical stimulation techniques and surgical intervention

According to Morris (2008) the reason for disruptive behaviours in the Secondary School in Lincolnshire in which this research was done is that: the school is a challenging comprehensive school in a selective LEA—thus students' levels of literacy problems are disproportionately high and fuel frustration among learners. Many of the school intake receive free school meals an indicator of social deprivation. At this school each year for the past five years, permanent exclusions have mounted to double figures. Also fixed term exclusions have fallen sharply yet numbers are still high. The school has a high rate of student mobility of 23.5%. There is also a legacy of poor public perception of the school in addition to parents are not always supportive. Many of our students bring a significant emotional 'baggage' to school on a daily basis. Attendance remains 'stubbornly low' (Ofsted 2006). A large number of the pupils claim they do not value education. Finally most of the pupils seem to have low self esteem.

Contemporary thinking

Whether the focus is on understanding behaviour and its effects by examining an individual's behavioural repertoire of itself, or the manner in which that behaviour is supported or sustained in different settings, a common approach now seems to be that any difficult behaviour is the result of the interaction between the individual and the environment. The emphasis tends to be on working from a positive attitude towards individuals (Cava 1990). In practical terms, this assumption implies a far-reaching and demanding stance, for example, it suggest that there has to be co-operation with others at international, national, regional and institutional levels to define and formulate shared values, behavioural standards and a behavioural code. The code should extend across the 'rights' responsibilities continuum; any arising charters and policies related to behaviour should be framed positively and optimistically, rather than in draconian form with the focus on just lists of sanctions.

Labels or categories for behaviour that becomes troublesome have to be better defined than they are currently; they need to refer explicitly to the nature of the behaviour, its antecedent and consequences; the manner and means by which adults regard each other and communicate with one another should model respect and value for the other party, a ready acceptance that the real meaning of any message in its day-to-day medium of transmission, in schools and elsewhere, is that it is no longer possible to adopt the 'do as I say, but not as I do' approach, it now has no credence; tackling difficult behaviour requires acting together so that behaviour does not become strongly reinforced because the responsible team or lead community, or some of its key members, pass the buck; acting together implies establishing agreement about the rules, the boundaries and the 'highway code' that should direct the management of behaviour.

Disruptive behaviour

Rogers (1998) postulated that every classroom has its share of disruptions. Of course they may be low-level disruptions, such as talking while the teacher is talking, seat-leaving, gum-chewing, calling out not having equipment, or uniform misdemeanour's. We no longer hear the respectful and dulcet tones of 'Please Sir', or 'Yes Miss'. More likely, we'll hear,' This work sucks', 'Gees this is boring,' 'You can't make me' and 'I don't care'. Add to this aggression, sulking, insolence, swearing and defiance, and it's easy to see why teaching is often rated as a highly stressful profession. There are times when students' reactions to the lessons are genuine because the teacher is inadequately prepared to deliver the lesson for various reasons. This might be to lack of experience as a teacher or lack experience in teaching the specific topic or a case of the teacher just did not take the time to plan. Sometimes teachers lack the necessary knowledge about the students they are teaching. It is very important that teachers have individual education plan for each student to see and know what their strengths and weaknesses are.

In this case when the reaction is genuine and the students are definitely bored because of lack of preparation the teacher will find it easy to amend this situation by simple planning carefully and properly. It is however very frustrating when having studied the individual education plan, carefully and proper planning is done to cater for all the students' need, the content is suitable, and the method is suitable but the pupils deliberately created a negative response. Normally starting with one or two students who decide they are going to ruin the lesson start to spread the notion that this lesson is boring or I am bored. Once one student starts this campaign, even the students who were focused and were a achieving the lesson objective become less focused and the teacher might lose them or they might not achieve the level they could possible achieve in a better psycho-social environment.

The causes of disruption

According to Rogers (1998) children disrupt for a number of reasons: boredom, fun, immaturity, inability to master the curriculum, low tolerance to frustration, or an emotionally disturbed and dysfunctional home situation. These days we are seeing more and more children whose home environment is seriously affecting their ability to cope in a formal' social setting like school. If Johnny's current male caregiver is unemployed, beats him regularly, has a drinking problem, if mum has five other children under 15, if there is regular screaming, shouting and put-downs at home, this will have an effect on Johnny's social behaviour at school. If he comes to school with significant inner conflict that he can hardly comprehend, and then meets an intransigent, petty teacher whose verbal repertoire is limited to hostile and embarrassing interaction, there is already a context for disruption. This is a particular bleak picture, but variations of this situation will be found in many schools.

Attention and audience

All human at some point seek attention and try to gain an audience. Even some genius who, history tells us that most of them tend to be very shy or introverted, work tireless to discover something new or to create something new. This in some ways is to gain attention or fame and to resultantly gain audience. According to Rogers, it is very evident at almost every level of school life, when a student comes into a group he immediately seeks to find some sort of 'social' place to belong. One of the central needs a person has is to be noticed, to be attended to and to have contact with others. Most students fulfil this need in socially acceptable ways. They put their hands up, they ask for equipment instead of snatching, they wait their turn, they gain positive attention through the production of acceptable work, they participate cooperatively—they 'belong. Their teachers and peers reinforce this acceptable mode of attention-seeking. It is this kind of behaviour that will allow the teacher to nurture students' potential into achieving their targets. This will lead to school also achieving their targets.

Primary and secondary behaviour

Rogers stated that another way of looking at attention-seeking behaviour is to view the behaviour cycle as progressive: from the primary disruption through to secondary attention—or power-seeking behaviours. A clear example used to illustrate this notion is—Cameron has secretly brought his expensive ultra-light Walk man into class and hidden the cassette deck in his bag by his feet. The teacher notices his nodding, hears the faint music and 'twigs'. She directs him to take it off and put it away; she addresses the primary behaviour. Now, Cameron does not say, 'Right Miss. I'll take it off straight away.' 'Thanks for pointing it out.' Cameron employs typical 'secondary' behaviours. He grunts, sighs to increase the feeling of 'notice how annoyed I am' and says, "gee, Miss Davies lets me play it in art class." Secondary behaviours include sighing, pouting, sulking behaviours and eyes rolled to the ceiling.

Students will sometimes answer back, procrastinate, or remove his hat in class. The student replies, 'Oh come on, (whine) other teachers don't care if we . . .' The reply, and the tone, and the body language are all secondary behaviour may be habitual, the result of frustration, or employed purposefully by the child. It may even be a teacher. Secondary behaviour can contribute to over-attendance by the teacher to the student (and over servicing), avoiding of responsibility for the real issue at stake—their primary behaviour (out of seat, calling out, having a comic on the desk, etc.), a feeling of guilt in the teacher, as if she shouldn't even be addressing the student about this behaviour. (This is where pouting, sighing, shoulder-shrugging, kicking-the-chair-in-passing are used for great effect as secondary behaviour—'I'll make you feel sorry'). This teacher is well-meaning, but through over-attention to Cameron's antics, her behaviour reinforces the thing she is trying to eliminate. Even if the child does stop disrupting (having got his dose of attention), it is likely he will employ similar behaviour next time he's after attention. Some children make a career of it. It's easy to fall into the trap of just reacting to such attention-seeking because we feel frustrated, angry, or anxious. What we often end up doing is just what the child wants—'Notice me', 'Attend to me when I want attention'.

The need for attention is fundamental in children, in all of us. It flows from the need to belong to a social group. It is very good that students are seeking attention. This is a very important aspect of the development of the individual becoming a person of worth and value. It is physically impossible for a teacher to give a class of say twenty-eight pupils the kind of attention they need to boost this level of confidence to develop this ability or sense of self. This is where I think more time and effort should be placed on the introduction of more classroom teaching assistance and other psychological support in modern schools. Too much is left to the teacher to respond to. This therefore means that something will prioritise and something will be left unattended. At times when the behaviour concerns are such that it cannot be ignored, the teacher has to intervene. This means that delivering the content becomes secondary when that should be the primary role of the teacher to ensure that students are educated on a specific topic. With the introduction of well educated learning support, this can be easily dealt with by them (teacher assistants) while the teacher carries on with the lesson. The teaching support can and should also be given the opportunity to record the behaviour of concern pupils on a class by class basis to be presented to other management for further disciplinary action.

Teacher Frustration

According to Rogers teachers will note how frustrated they get with children when they call out, make silly noises, tap and the like. This is both a problem and a clue for what we can do when dealing with such behaviour. Because we are frustrated by the child's behaviour (Attend to me', Spend time on me', Engage the group to notice me') it is easy to act in accord with the child's goal. In fact, the child may have learned how to trigger such attention from adults even if such attention is adult anger. 'Gee I can get him angry just by calling out or I can make him come over to me by pleading.' Some children may not be consciously aware of their attention-seeking or power-struggling behaviour, even if the attention is negative in tone or manner. It is essential in dealing with such behaviours to marshal thoughtful discipline responses.

Rogers postulated that power seeking is another form of attention-seeking. The power-seeking child is out to 'belong' by using challenging behaviour: 'can't make me ', 'not gonna do this work', 'This work is boring', 'I hate you', and 'I don't care anyway'. When such a child throws out a challenge, he is inviting the teacher to a contest. His belief may even register as 'I belong when I'm as powerful or more powerful than the teacher' or 'I must win, she must lose'. When the teacher uses more force—'You'll do this work or else,' she endorses the child's purposeful behaviour.

There is also the added problem that there is sense in which a teacher cannot make a child do any work. She can invite, ask, direct, apply consequences but cannot merely make. We can, of course, make a small child move from one place to another by physically 'moving' him, but we can hardly do that with a robust year 7 student who responds by saying, 'No, I'm not going to move and you can't make me.' What are we going to do? Drag him out? Fight him? There are more effective ways of dealing with power-seeking students than merely giving them the easy win-lose perspective they seek. Power seeking children 'feed' off force, which is why it makes good sense to avoid such a reaction. The teacher's response (rather than reaction) can reinforce a child's inappropriate behaviour as much as anything else.

Awareness of disruptive behaviour patterns

If we are aware that some children's misbehaviour is purposeful in seeking attention or an exchange of power, we can better plan how to manage disruptions that arise from behaviour. If a child is actively seeking attention in off-task, clownish, annoying ways, it is counter-productive to let him achieve such at the expense of our frustration: 'I won't tell you again, just sit down will you.' If we are aware of the behaviour that signals attention-seeking, we need to be consciously prepared not to over-attend or fall into power exchanges. If Johnny is purposefully baiting the teacher with a whining 'This work sucks', it is clear that an angry retort from the teacher will only reinforce such behaviour. This child may never have successfully learned cooperative ways to belong but he gets an 'A' for being a 'pain'. We may be the ones giving the marks. Effective disciplinary approaches will seek to minimise a child's inappropriate ways of belonging through attention-seeking and power-play, and maximise appropriate ways to belong. The way we do this will depend on our teaching style and what skills we bring to bear. Such skills need to be developed in a planned and purposeful way. The combination rarely occurs accidental.

Behaviour problems and causal mechanisms

Since the early 1960s, the Mental Health Programme of the World Health Organisation has been actively engaged in improving the diagnosis and classification of mental disorders. Thus, ICD—10 (WHO 1992) contains a group of disorders described as 'Behavioural and Emotional Disorders with onset usually occurring in childhood and adolescence' and includes 'Conduct Disorders', Hyperkinetic Disorders', 'Disorders of Social Functioning' and so on. Severe problem behaviour in schools is most often associated with conduct disorders and characterised by a repetitive and persistent pattern of antisocial aggressive or defiant conduct such as disobedience, provocative behaviour severe temper tantrums, excessive fighting or bullying, cruelty, destructiveness, stealing, lying, truancy and fire setting. 5.3 per cent of children were found to have conduct disorder in a recent survey (Meltzer et al 2000). These problems are not only common, but are also persistent, difficult to treat, expensive for the society and have poor prognosis (Kazdin 1993, Robins 1991).

Conduct disorders are generated and maintained by a large number of factors in a variety of ecologically nested systems. Important social factors include involvement with deviant peers, drug abuse and psychosocial adversity such as overcrowding, institutional care and so on. Family factors include a family history of criminal behaviour, violence at home, use of physical methods of punishment, child abuse, coercive parenting, ineffective parental monitoring and supervision, providing inconsistent consequences for rule violations, failing to provide reinforcement for pro-social behaviour, family disorganisation, attachment difficulties, marital discord, and so on. School factors include being a 'failing' school, with discipline problems, attainment difficulties, and lack of educational resources. Individual factors include difficult temperament, early separation experience, Attention Deficit Hyperactivity Disorder, hostile attribution bias (perceiving hostile intention in others' ambiguous actions), poor social skills, poor learning of pro-social behaviour from experience, academic underachievement and learning difficulties.

The multiplicity of causative factors has also promoted a number of theories that explain the mechanisms. For example, the sociological theory of 'Anomie' highlights the illegitimate means used by members of a socially disadvantaged delinquent subculture to achieve material goals valued by mainstream culture (Cloward and Ohlin 1960). System theories emphasise the role of characteristics of various systems (for example, family system, broader social network and social systems) in the causation and maintenance of behaviour problems, for example, confusing and unclear rules, roles routines and communication in a family or a school. Social learning theories examine the role of modelling and reinforcements. Thus, behaviour problems may arise owing to imitation of others, for example, parents, siblings, peers, teachers, and media characters) behaviours. Many children learn to continue their peer group. Parents or teachers can also reinforce (often negatively) such behaviours by confronting or punishment and the child learns that the escalation of antisocial behaviour leads to parental or teacher's withdrawal.

Similarly, in these behaviour situations, there are cognitive theories. In social situations where the intentions of others are ambiguous, children with conduct disorder tend to exit aggressive behaviour. According to social informal processing theory, this is intended to be retaliatory because they attribute hostile intentions to others in such situations (Crick and Dodge 1994). According to Social Skills Deficit Theory, children with conduct disorder lack the skills to generate alternative solutions to social problems and to implement such solutions

Characteristics of the classroom

Wearmouth, Richmond, Glyn (2004) postulated that:

- Classrooms are busy places. Teachers can be engaged in 1000 interactions a day, and in some cases, sometimes more. It is very difficult to name a comparable job on this dimension: perhaps traffic controllers cope with comparable complexity, although their job makes less personal demands. Teachers make a non-trivial decision in the classroom every two minutes.
- Classrooms are public places. This statement is meant in two ways. First classroom **are** public in the general sense that many people have a view

or opinion on classrooms and how they ought to operate. Second, classrooms are public in that a teacher's and a student's behaviour is generally highly visible to all the other members in the event.

- Classroom events are multi-dimensional. There is a wide variety of purposes, interests and goals represented by the different persons in a classroom. The teacher may have thoughts about the staff meeting this evening, or the students may have thoughts about what is on television or what someone said to their friend. In the middle of this, teaching and learning takes place. Personal-social aspects of pupils' and teachers lives are always affecting classroom life. Even when we focus on the learning dimension alone the statement still applies. The classroom contains a multiplicity of information sources—books, worksheets, displays, other visuals, as well as all the verbal and non-verbal behaviour of teachers and students and these sources generally do not all refer to the same thing.

- Classroom events are simultaneous. The multiple events in the classroom do not occur in a step-by-step fashion but simultaneously, especially from the teacher's point of view. One group is happily working away, another group wants attention for something, and meanwhile someone is climbing out of the window.

- Classroom events are unpredictable. In such a busy, multidimensional environment it is not possible to be in a position of predicting the course of events with a fine degree of accuracy. Despite teachers' proper professional attempts to predict how a group might respond to the material, or how long it might take, they know that there will be surprises, so they generally become skilled in recognizing and tolerating unpredictability. This helps to recognise the poverty of those views which portray the classroom as a simple cause-and-effect situation, which offer a simple teacher-centred view, and which seem to imply that there is a prescription for successful teaching in all contexts. These views are common, but are positively dangerous as a basis for improving classrooms.

The most effective element in reducing general classroom disruption is the teacher's skill in planning activities. This implication is supported by research findings such as those of Kounin (1977), who's extensive and detailed studies showed that the action which teachers took in response to a discipline problem had no consistent relationship with their managerial success in the classroom.

Styles of responding

Wearmouth, Richmond, and Glyn in response to the fact that Tim took a student's ruler the more able teacher will use a positive approach to deal with the situation. Tim you're quite able to get on with your work, so return Rosemary's ruler and let her do the same. Rather than in a confrontational demanding way say give back the ruler. De-escalation is a commonly used term in our schools today. It is far much better to try to de-escalate every behaviour situation if one would like to get the best result. In order to avoid a negative secondary behaviour, the teacher should try to find something positive or friendly to say to the student before addressing the primary behaviour. "Tim you look quite smart today," "That is a very nice shoe you are wearing today" and you can put a little smile on his face. This will destroy his plan of reacting negatively therefore; in essence you are actually taking him by surprise. The element of surprise is always important when dealing with behaviour. It is after getting him in a communicative mode then it is possible to ask him to return the ruler. It is also important not to embarrass when doing this by taking away the feeling of power from him so the teacher should give him time to react and also walk away. The word please should always be used when making a request from a student and also to say thanks even before they actual carry out the positive act. This will teach pupil how to conduct themselves.

Teachers' way of conveying to pupils that behaviour is inappropriate

Hargreaves, Hester and Mellor (1975) identified the following 11 teacher strategies:

- Descriptive statement of the deviant conduct: 'You're taking a long time to settle down'.
- Statement of the rule which is being invoked: 'Rulers aren't for fighting with', 'When I'm talking no one else talks'.
- Appeal to pupil's knowledge of the rule: 'You know you're meant to write it in the book'.
- Command/ request for conformity to the rule: 'Shut up', 'Put that away'.
- Prohibitions: 'Don't', 'Stop that'.
- Questions: 'Are you listening?', 'What's going on over there?'
- Statement of the consequences of the deviant conduct:' I won't bother to read if you go on like

this', 'Someone will get hurt if this equipment is left lying here'

- Warnings and threats: 'I'm going to get annoyed', 'You'll be in detention', 'I'll send you to the head'.
- Evaluate labels of the pupil and her or his conduct: 'Stop behaving like a baby', 'Don't be daft'.
- Sarcasm: 'We can do without the singing', 'Have you retired?'
- Attention-drawers: 'Sandra', 'Girls'.

It is believed that strategies 2 and 7 are worthy of our attention since they achieve two goals. They signal that the behaviour is unwanted and they communicate the rule which the teacher sees as being broken. As such they are likely to have the most effective long-term contribution, especially in a classroom where the communication of informal rules seems to have been ineffective. Within this theme we do not want to convey an image of successful classrooms as rule-bound environments: neither pupils nor teachers find that motivating, and the occasions when rules are relaxed are often memorable for building relationships. One of students' criteria for judging teachers is Can he have a laugh (Gannaway, 1984). However, breaking rules are most meaningful when someone knows what the rule is that is being broken.

Skills in Managing the Classroom Context

Wearmouth, Richmond, Glyn (2004) stated that creative teachers display many skills. Those included in the following framework relate to the particular complexities of the classrooms which were outlined at the start of this chapter. They postulated that there should be proper management of the following:

- Physical setting—layout, seating, resources, etc.
- Managing the social structure—groupings, working pattern etc.
- Managing the psychological setting of the classroom—handling the timing and pacing, developing effective routines, giving a personal yet public performance, with a focus on group participation, being aware of the multiple dimensions of classroom life and showing it, managing more than one event at the same time, and recognizing and tolerating the unpredictable nature of classroom life.

Classroom rules and routines

Wearmouth, Richmond, Glyn (2004) postulated that rules in the classrooms are not operative just because the teacher says so. They have to be set up, agreed, used and periodically re-examined. This is not a once-and-for-all process. Routines also make a contribution. They may not be framed as a 'rule', but they are the way of making regular events happen. These may take the form of how resources are accessed, how homework is handed in, how the classroom is entered and so on. The purpose of any rule or routine needs to be clarified in the way it is framed and through review with the class. The steps which they recommended for effectiveness are:

- Establishing—needs a lot of communication / teaching at the early stage.
- Agreeing—pupils are likely to agree if rules are few in number and their purpose is clear.
- Using—all parties need to publicize and refer to the rules, and mediate them in so doing.
- Reviewing—periodically the class examines whether the rules in use are fulfilling their purpose. According to Hargreaves, Hester and Mellor (1975), this may include talk, movement, time, teacher-pupil relationships and pupil-pupil relationships.

The language of Behaviour Management

The manner in which each behavioural concerns are dealt with is very important. Wearmouth, Richmond,

Glyn (2004) classify this as the language of behaviour. They postulated that one should keep the corrective interaction intrusive wherever possible. For example, we can manage such behaviours and issues as calling out, lateness, learning chairs, uniform misdemeanours and students without equipment with 'low' intrusion. It important to avoid unnecessary confrontation this includes embarrassment, any sarcasm invokes hostility and resentment. It is imperative to keep a respectful, positive tone of voice wherever possible. It is also very important to keep the language itself positive where possible. One should always remember to re-establish working relationship with the pupils as quickly as possible. One must always try to communicate appropriate frustration, for example anger, assertively as possible and not aggressively, making it as brief as possible. It is very important to follow up on issues that matter beyond the classroom context. This will emphasise and show that you, the teacher, care enough about the issues and concerns of the student.

Teacher bullying (students who bully teachers) a case study

According to Rogers (2000) it was the ghastly note that finally pushed her 'over the edge'. For many weeks she had been bottling up her anxiety and her frustration—she had hoped it would go away. It didn't. The year 9 pupil was bulling her—almost 'stalking' her. The way he stared at her and eye balled her and the accidental look as he walked past her. Then it was the comments—the snide comments about her clothes and her physical appearance. In other instances, it was the comments he made in class out loud, that could garner the pathetic laughter of his little compliant coterie. Most of his comments were made when others were around so that teacher (who was already clearly flustered and unfocused when this student was in the room) couldn't always be sure who said it.

Like most bullies, he perceived in the teacher a weakness of character or personality that he could manipulate to his advantage. He had it in his head that this teacher was fair game and even deserved it-'it' being his ability to hurt others he felt were not ok. Such is the twisted logic of a bully. He watched to see the increasing effect of his 'look', his words and his manipulation of the group. Like a gun firing bullets, he could sabotage a lesson by sending out non-verbal cues to other members in the class who would also comment, disrupt a lesson or refuse to comply with a teacher request. He 'fired the gun' and sat back and watched his 'bullets' do the work. No doubt (like gutless wonders) he felt the power of control, a perfect example of what bulling is all about. The abuse of relational power (Rogers 1995) and the distorted and damaging control exercised by a person who believes he or she is more powerful, psychologically or physically, than the person selected to bully. The trouble was that she had let the insidious comments, the corridor laughter, the non-verbal signals that indicated physical acts, the group's silence as she walked past and then the laughter, and the whispered comments, go on and on. But the passing of a note was the culmination. She had seen him pass it. It was disgusting. She had found the note by accident on the floor after class. She'd recognised his writing though he hadn't signed it. She took it to the co-ordinator after weeks of personal torment. Finally something was done to resolve the matter out. The student was confronted and suspended. By then the psychological damage had been done.

Recommendation

According to B. F. Skinner's theory which is based on Operant Conditioning the organism is in the process of "operating" on the environment, which in ordinary terms means it is bouncing around its world, doing what it does. During this "operating," the organism encounters a special kind of stimulus, called a reinforcing stimulus, or simply a reinforcer. This special stimulus has the effect of increasing the operant, that is, the behaviour occurring just before the reinforcer. This is operant conditioning: "the behaviour is followed by a consequence, and the nature of the consequence modifies the organism's tendency to repeat the behaviour in the future."

A behaviour followed by a reinforcing stimulus results in an increased probability of that behaviour occurring in the future.

A behaviour no longer followed by the reinforcing stimulus results in a decreased probability of that behaviour occurring in the future.

A behaviour followed by an aversive stimulus results in a decreased probability of the behaviour occurring in the future.

With respect to B F Skinner theory on operant conditioning, organisms are given rewards for positive or for displaying an acceptable behaviour. I am very supportive of this notion and would recommend for a Secondary School in Lincolnshire a 'Happy Hour Programme'. This would be a one hour period at the end of each school day where students select a sports or computer session (game site) of their choice and develop competitions on a house basis. This should be carefully developed by doing a survey to ascertain the activities that the students are mostly interested in. The entire school population should be involved in this programme and information about the daily winners should be placed on the school's notice board. In addition, names of the monthly winners should be placed on the school's website and school magazines. The winners could be labelled "Stars of the day."

The chance to participate in the Happy Hour programme should be a privilege and not a right. Hence, it is a system of merit. If a student is on a detention from any lesson of the day, they will not go to the happy hour session but they will sit in a classroom and do one extra hour of what ever subject they were detained for. It should be a very disciplined programme and as such if a student has a sports final to play, they should not be allowed to play. The student who has completed a day successfully without getting any detention would achieved this fantastic happy hour. This will help to improve the psycho-social environment and the ethos of the school in a manner to make students more actively involved and feel apart of the institution. In addition, it will also help teachers to get a chance socialize with their pupils in a different setting; hence students will be able to view their teachers from a different perspective.

I have discovered that there is a gender difference with respect to behaviour as well. In some ways the females and the males in lower ability groups at the secondary school in Lincolnshire tend to behave differently. I think the females are more personal with their behaviour, by this I meant they tend to attack teachers with unkind verbal comments and and also seek more level of attention and audience. Conversely the males are different in that they tend to be loud, play music, never have equipment and sometimes damage equipment spitefully. Based on the difference in behaviour patterns I would recommend that in the lower ability groups where disruptive behaviours are more prevalent that there is a gender split. This means that females should be placed in different groups from males. This will give the teacher a chance to deal with a specific kind of behaviour. Consequently teachers will be better able to become specialist in dealing with a particular kind of behaviour if more time is spent on dealing with one level of disruption.

It is a given that some teachers are better at dealing with behaviour than some. This may be for different reasons, for example the amount of experience in the classroom, amount of effort placed in learning to understand students' behaviour and what technique or strategy works for each individual, the level of relationship and support that teacher can get from parent. Whatever it is that makes the teacher more superior in dealing with behaviour, this should be developed and shared among all members of staff. Consequently I recommend that there be more sessions across the school faculties where teachers are able to discuss strategies and technique that work best for a particular student. There could possible be data base where these strategies are stored for teachers, and especially new teachers therefore given them the opportunity to get it right as soon as possible,

At this Secondary school the parents are involve in the lives of the pupils and tend to offer support when necessary. This is a positive ground on which to build a better extended school community. I recommend sessions for parents where they are given the chance to be educated as to what are the objectives and targets of the school, what are preventing the school from achieving these targets, and have them suggest ways of dealing with these issues. The problem of behaviour should be brought to the forefront. This will give rise to the opportunity for the school and the parents to strengthen alliance in dealing with behaviour concerns. Students will tend to feel that it is impossible for them to win when they see a combination of effort from school and home. The same value system at school is replicated at home.

Finally like students, teachers need motivation and reinforcement for good behaviour, good practice, and good attitude. Based on this notion I would recommend for this secondary school more social functions for the staff, where staff members are given awards for their effort. This can have a very positive effect on staff and hence motivate them to perform better. It is possible that some staff might feel unhappy with this but careful planning and honesty can prevent any staff from feeling unfairly treated. A motivated, mentally fit and physically fit staff will be better able to carry out their roles and function in a more confident and effective way. The students we teach can easily see when the teacher are confident in whatever they are doing and knowledgeable in what they are saying.

Cooper, Smith and Upton (1994 p.75) suggested that a behavioural approach looks outside the child to the classroom environment and experiences to find ways of changing behaviour . . . any problems are the teacher's responsibility not the child's fault. Consequently I would like to conclude that whatever the behaviour is, the following should be considered:

- Knowledge about the behaviour the history of it the biological nature.
- Careful planning in order to respond correctly
- Support from parents and other member of staff.
- The use of the word 'we'
- Confident and motivated approach by staff when dealing with behavioural concerns

Reinforcements for acceptable behaviours and conversely aversive stimulation for unacceptable behaviours will have some effect on modifying behaviour. In addition to list of important aforementioned ideas, it is very important that the teacher knows the school policies and the national policies and be very consistent when using them. Finally, learning is what brings about a change in behaviour, so until the student finally learns that he will be rewarded positively for his good behaviour but punished for this bad behaviour, then there will be no change in behaviour.

Bibliography:

Erikson, E., Identity Youth and Crisis.
London: Faber and Faber
Erikson, E., 1972 Young Man Luther.
London: Faber and Faber.
Rogers, B., 1998 You Know The Fair Rule
England: Financial Times Prentice Hall
Rogers, B., Cracking The Hard Class.
London: Paul Chapman Publishing Ltd
Rogers, B., 1998 You Know The Fair Rule
England: Financial Times Prentice Hall
Rogers, B., Cracking The Hard Class.
London: Paul Chapman Publishing Ltd
Warriner, J., 1986 English Grammar and Composition
Orlando: Harcourt Brace Jovanovich, Publishers
Wearmouth, J., Richmond, R., Glyn, T., and Berryman, M., 2004 Understanding Pupils Behaviour in Schools.
London: David Fulton Publishers Ltd.
Wearmouth, J., Richmond, R., and Glyn, T., 2004 Addressing Pupils' Behaviour.
London: David Fulton Publishers Ltd
Wearmouth, J., Richmond, R., Glyn, T., and Berryman, M., 2004 Inclusion and Behaviour Management in Schools
London: David Fulton Publishers Ltd.

References :

Smith, C., Confrontation In The Classroom

Bob, Sproson., Teacher Effectiveness in Managing Behaviour.

Skinner, B., Personility Theories Publish by Boeree, G.,2006 www.ship.edu/~cgboeree/skinner.html—

Strategies for Changing Behaviour

Senco week<senco-week@senco.teachingexpertise.com

To Be Or Not To Be

The father of light wants to raise you up into the heavens at no cost no charge, the only thing that is required is for you is to claim your seat in the elevator. How do you claim your seat in the elevator? It is so simple you would not believe it. All you need to do is to say "I want to be lifted up" and mean this with all your heart and mind. Did you know about the fact that the father of light has already prepared a place for us all where we can live in happiness and luxury? It is called the heavens. You don't have to die to live up in the heavens where there is no sin, just joy. Consider yourself driving your new truck. How amazing does it look and how fantastic it is with speed. But on this particular day, when you tried to drive off you realized that the more you pressed on the accelerator the truck still would not increase in speed. It maintained the same slow miserable undesirable speed. This was at a time when you really wanted to get off to work because you actually woke up late.

You started to get frustrated and you cursed the truck. You wished you had bought a different truck. This is not heaven, this is something else called frustration. The heaven that the father of light spoke about is a calm positive mental attitude that is in your mind. You don't have to die to experience the heavens. As soon as you become calm and think constructively and reflect you would have remembered that the night before you pulled up the hand brake. The father of light is always there to elevate you up into the heavens. Just listen to the calm whispering voice. You then released the handbrake and the truck sped off. How does this make you feel? You are in the heavens. You are in a life of joy. Things are happening for you. The fact that the truck did not move off at first was for a reason or more than one reasons. It might be that you needed to calm down before you went on the road or you might have been in an accident. Maybe it was just a lesson for the day to say please be extra careful and think through things before taking any action. So don't think that up in the heavens you are not going to have these moments. It is only the people who can see that they are there for a reason are the true angels of the light and as such can live a life of praise.

Cherish these moments because you have just been protected by the father of light. You are blessed. Eventually you will see that nothing happens accidentally. Everything is ordained to protect and serve you because you are an angel. A king is born. As you protect and serve, so will you be protected. Everything that you do on earth is rewarded in the heavens. If you spend your life protecting and serving, then your reward is going to be great because the angels above will be doing the same for you. If you make someone happy then the angels will make you happy. This is automatic. It is a principle of life. A king is born. Do you understand the concept of a principle? A principle will work anywhere. For example, if you throw a piece of paper in the sky it will come back down. This is a simple principle that will work in any language, it doesn't matter where you are. If your life as a king is to protect and serve, then you will be protected and served by the father of light. Live your life on that principle. Make sure that you understand that whatever happens is just an experience, it is just a lesson to help you move on and it happened to protect you from a greater danger. It is also preparing you for a greater victory.

A victory is coming. You will need to borrow a donkey's jawbones to help you to laugh. Prepare to laugh and give praise. A greater joy is coming. This is the principle of life. Your great day of joy is coming. When I was a little boy growing up in my community, I used to be fooled by some of the elders. When we were having happy times, they would say to us that we are too happy. They would say that when one is too happy, something bad is going to happen. This would eventually happen because we were led to believe this. They planted a sour seed in our minds. When we were happy, we would prepare for something sad to happen. Having met the father of light, I realised that this was far from the truth. Anything that happens is just to protect from harming yourself.

ALTRUISM IS HEART OF A GOOD KING

Everyday a king is born but not every king that is born goes on to sit on a throne. Not all of them even get to know that they are kings. We live in a world that is lacking important knowledge or maybe the necessary knowledge is not shared with all of us. Only some people are privy to this important body of information. Do we know for a fact that in the Garden of Eden in the book of Genesis that God spoke to Adam and Eve? Do we know the words that were spoken by the father of light at creation? It is a given that there must be a body of knowledge somewhere that is important to guide all men. If each man heals another man, then all men would be healed. There is no difference between men apart from their level of knowledge, their environment, and their level of training. I have met the father of light. His words were that he came onto his own and his own received him not, but as many as received him, to them he gave the powers to become sons of the light. A king is born.

Many are called but few are chosen. The choice to be chosen is up to you. If you treat yourself like a slave, people will treat you like a slave. If you treat yourself very low, people will treat you very low. If you treat yourself like a prince, people will treat you like a prince. If you treat yourself like a kin, people will accept you and treat you like a king. If you continue to live this way, soon you will establish your throne far and wide until the world accepts you this way. Your family will eventually become a royalty and the tradition will go on and on forever. A king is born. Anything you say about yourself can become true. If you say you are silly you will feel and act silly. If you say that you will never be able to do something then that will become true. If on the contrary you say positive things about yourself then this will become true.

Throughout your lifetime you will never live to understand the full capacity and capability of the brain. We all have photographic memories. If we say that we have photographic memories, then we will have photographic memories. Life and death is in the power of the tongue. Whatever we say about ourselves is true. If we say that we are sick then we will become sick. Hear no evil nor speak no evil. The things that we hear will become a part of our thinking so be careful of what you listen to. If you feed your mind with garbage then you will think garbage. If you feed your mind with thistles and thorns then your whole life will be full of thistles and thorns. Speak about the things that you want in life and not the things that you do not want. The evil things that you wish for other people will become a part of your life. If you wish bad things for other people then this will happen to you. Speak no evil. Let the father of light shine through you and then you will speak of the light. The offenders will have their time when they attack you. If you have to attack, just attack them, but when the war is over it is over. Wish them all the best and move on.

WHO ARE YOU

I am a giant killer. Do you remember the story about David and Goliath? Everyone thought that this big monster would slew this poor little shepherd boy. David on the contrary was thinking that he was a giant killer. The giants in our lives are those major problems or challenges that we face everyday. Plan your attack on your giants. It does not matter what the plan is, as long as you attack them one by one.

Never feel that you will get rid of all your giants. It is therefore important to feel that giant killing is a part of your life. This is what makes you into a strong and confident adult. You have to get to that point in your life where you enjoy killing your giants. Don't be afraid of your giants. Don't think that if you attack your giants you are going to die. Take the steps to attack your giants. There was a man who was so afraid of dying that he stayed in his room and refused to go outside because of his fear that something would happen to him that might take his life. He fell off his bed one day and hit his head and died. Don't be afraid of facing your giants.

ALL QUEEN WILL NOW BE HAPPY

Making your queen happy is a very important task because when the Queen is happy, the whole kingdom is happy. Do you have to be a "yes man" at all times for the Queen to be happy? The Queen will be happy if the children are happy. It is therefore imperative to make all the children happy and the Queen will be eventually happy. The queen will always be the queen. They should always have something to look forward to. Never try to control a queen. It is in the act of never trying to control a queen that they will be yours. For everyday she rises, she must rise into a new world and if she does rise in the same world twice she will wonders off. Creating a new world for your queen every day is an easy feat. Some people call it dangling the carrot, while dangling the carrot is good. We have to remember that the queen always want to achieve and show independence and character. Simple allow and create avenues for this every day and the queen will be happy.

THE PRICE YOU HAVE TO PAY

A king is born. Nothing in life is free. Nothing will come without a price. The big question therefore is 'is the price worth it? When I was a small boy my father always tell me that if you were born a male you were born a man, and as such, you have to be treated differently because you are a man. He also once told me about a bird he called chicken hawk. He said that they have the best theories to life and this is how a man should be treated. The chicken hawk's theory is that as soon as its little infant start feathering, the hawk would take them far into the sky and let them go. The ones who were able to fly would live and those who were not able to fly would die. This he said is how life is. The fittest of the fittest will survive.

I later read Charles Darwin's Theory which basically said the same thing that weak people will not survive in this world, only the strong will survive. I am strong, I survived his test. I am a king. I have overcome my giants. I am not afraid of my giants. I remember one day we were in the woods with him and we were attacked by a large wild boar. I started to run but my dad did not because he was thinking that the boar could be good food for the rest of the month. He attacked the boar and slew it. We had pork for the month. I later asked him if he was scared when we were attacked and he told me that he was not because he was prepared. He told me to "always expect the unexpected." One should never look scared when confronting the enemy. Look straight into their eyes and plan to fight to the very end. Never look scared.

TOUCHED BY THE MASTER

In my teaching career while working in Jamaica I have had good times and bad times. I had moments that brought tears to my heart eyes. I remember one night I was in my room and a scorpion attacked me in my dream. Because I am not a very fearful person, my first reaction was to kill it. I tried to kill it but it ran away. I searched all night but I could not find it. This created mixed feelings and thoughts in me. The fact that it did not sting me was good. The fact that it is still out there alive was bad because this meant that it could come again. This however made me stronger because I was able to mentally prepare for the unknown. Always prepare for the unexpected. I was strengthened and protected by the fact that I did not show any sign of fear. This gave me the courage to prepare for the unknown. I am now more than ever prepare mentally and physically for whatever that will happen. I am also trying constantly to create my own path. Even though I have to comply with rules and regulation and codes and practices I am trying to make my own world during the confines of the work world. A king is born.

The father of light has blessed me with many amazing lessons to guide me in my teaching career. One such amazing lesson was the incident with the lady who sinned and was about to be stoned to death. This was the law of the land. Everyone was ready to stone her to death. The Father of Light appeared and questioned the mob about what they were doing. Like every teacher, I thought this was a very difficult moment for the father of light but his words were so simple and effective. He instructed that he who is without sin should cast the first stone. No one could do so. This is because at some point in our life we have all made mistakes. Though this seem very strong, I use this lesson to always guide me to remember that no matter what bad things a student do it is not unique to them and that it is humane to err and to forgive is divine. My job is not to write off a pupil but to search for a quality and capitalise on it and nurture it. It is my duty to set them free and guide them to the path of success. I had a student in my lesson who was a Rastafarian. His locks were very neat and clean and really looked nice. He was admired by most of the females in his class and because of this he almost lost his way academically. One day I asked him what would he like to be ten years from now. He did not have a plan. He was just going through the motion of attending school. I must say that some people will feel good and bad about what I have done because they might think that I have sent someone into a profession for the wrong reasons. While this might be true, I have seen many youths with potential who have totally wasted their time. The bad thing is that they not only waste their time alone, but they have also wasted the time of others.

I was confident that by the time he completes his training he would get very serious about his life. There was no sense of direction in this powerful young king. I told him that I could see that he was fascinated by girls. I told him that I wanted him to research the work of gynaecologists and then find ten of the most famous gynaecologist in the world and visit me in two weeks. The rest is history. He is now a medical student at the University of the West Indies. Touch by the master's hand, I am sure that those who are passionate about the work they do have magical powers that affect their jobs in an extremely positive way. I have seen many good male barbers with long hair that they don't trim. They treasure their hair. I have even seen some Rastafarian men doing barbering. Rastafarians are people whose faith holds the principle that a man should grow his hair. People who have a passion for hair have magical power of how to care for hair. Find talents in people and help them to establish themselves.

KING OF WAR.

They should never know when you will strike. The element of surprise is important. When you are weak, make them feel that you are strong. When you are strong, you are ready if they attack, so make them feel that you are week. Again the element of surprise will take effect. A king is born.

A Man Who Hid His Money in the Bush.

A man won the lottery one day and went up into the hills and hid his money under a tree. After hiding the money, he took a picture of the tree to remember the exact spot. He then went away to celebrate his victory in a very far land. On the third day of his trip, he decided to take a look at the picture he took where he hid his money. As he took out his camera and looked at the picture, to his dismay there was a man in the tree smiling. He was so shocked he did not even realise who it was. Suddenly his phone rang and it was his son. He then asked him "Did you see my face in the picture?" His son told him not to worry because he knew that his dad always forget things so I followed him to ensure that everything went ok. He told his dad that his secret was safe with him. He was now so relieved.

Proverbs

Don't jump into the water if you can't swim. If you know that your shoulders are not broad enough you should never go into something or into a situation before getting the necessary training and preparation When the time is right, then go forth and conquer. It is always important to aim for the top and aim for the sky, but this however, must be done tactfully and done after careful consideration. Make sure you have devised a plan and you have carefully studied your plan. At this point, you are ready to jump in the water because you can swim. It is important that you look at this situation; however this best way for me to express this situation is to share this story with you. There was a pond filled with crocodiles in a small village. The pond contained some of the most dangerous crocodiles and there were hundreds of them.

One day there was a competition in the village and it was that someone should swim across the pond that contained the very dangerous and hungry crocodiles. The winner of the competition would become a King in the village. On the day of the competition, all the media representatives gathered. When the announcer took the microphone, before he could finish his welcoming speech, a little old man swam across the pond in a flash. When the announcer ran up to him to congratulate him, he furiously said "You are talking about a prize, I am looking for the person who pushed me off." The old man did not swim across on his own because a little boy pushed him off. Fortunately he made it across the pond safely and received the honour. The point I am making is that even if you jump in the water and you can't swim, just swim. So, although it is said don't jump in the water if you can't swim, if you are in the water don't give up. You will do it if you try.

THE SKY IS THE LIMIT.

When I understood what this wise saying meant my heart almost raced out of my chest. If the sky is the limit, there is no limit because the limit to the sky. When you think about how much money you can make if you don't limit yourself to a job but expand yourself as large and wide as you can, spread your wings and fly. You will see that there is no limit to what you can earn. The limit to what you can earn is defined by you. A king is born. My earning power has no limit. My success has no limits. I am going to take it to the sky. Someone once told me that I am high. I am above the sky

When You have the Instrument of Influence Using with Sense.

Many people strive for leadership positions and when they receive it they abuse the people who they lead. They tend to forget that they were once in that same position as the person who they lead. They can't show empathy to the mass who they lead. They miss their calling. They don't know that to lead means to serve. If you are a king, you are a big servant serving the mass. If you empower those around you, they will learn the concept of building people, so they will go on to develop others as well. Soon you will have a large network of people who will look up to you as their leader. This can happen all the time if you are a leader who uses your instruments of influence with sense. On the contrary, if you try to tear down the people that you lead, they will try to tear you down as well. This leaves the possibility that one day you can be out of power and there will be no one to help you. If you help people to make it to the top, then you will have a network that will look after you for life. Teach people how to fish, don't give them a fish. If you teach them how to fish for themselves, they will come to you and offer you a fish when you are down.

No Procrastination, Know The True Value of Time.

When I was going to school as a student I had this experience. This is an experience that I will never forget. Once I had an important exam to do. I really wanted to get a good grade so I told myself that I would start my studying two months before the exam. I keep putting off my studies until the last two days. Unfortunately the night before the exam, electricity went away so I could not study. I went into the exam the following day very unprepared. Although I did not fail, I swam even when I did not plan to swim. I did not however get the best mark in the exam. This affected me because I was placed in a lower group. A king is born. Know the true value of time. Time that is lost cannot be regained. If you sit and calculate how much time you have wasted not doing anything, you would be surprised. Do not procrastinate if you are the kind of person who is trying to reach the top.

Working for thirteen hours

I once had a job that I did on weekends. I had to stand in an arcade for thirteen hours checking and shining machines and ensuring that no one messed with the machines. Thirteen hours were very long and stressful and the pay for doing this job was very low. On many occasions I used to be confronted by people who were close to me asking me why I continue to destroy myself. At times I would also ask myself the same question. I know that the little money that I got for my pay helped to pay some bills but apart from that it was stressful. I had to work very regularly in a section they called the high licence. This was a very lonely section so I had a very long time to sit and meditate. Sometimes three hours would pass before a gambler would come in and spend twenty or thirty minutes and then go.

During this time I met with the father of light. I was told by the father of light that this was just a character building process. I explored all possible fields with the father of light and he took me on a long journey. He led me to the gates of heaven and then told me if I want to enter the choice was mine and that I should just act. I realised that what people need in life is not a job but a career. When you do something that you love, you don't see it as work because you have fun and earn.

You can only perform at maximum if you are happy. Remember that happiness brings success not success brings. Find something that you love to do and make it into a career. When you have a career you will realize that you do not need to keep looking at the clock every time. You are in control. When you have a job similar to the thirteen hours shift job similar to the one I had you are not in control of any department of your life. You work so hard and then you can't even find enough to enjoy yourself.

FOR FAITH WITHOUT WORKS IS VAIN

I can achieve it if I believe it. It is important to have faith and tell others about your faith. It has been written that if you have faith as small as a mustard seed, you can remove a mighty mountain. I have never seen a mountain move without some action. So don't always think that when it was said that faith without works is vain people are saying that you should go and do a thirteen hours shift. Sometimes it is just the act of speaking the word. What is important though is that we act. In creation, it has been said that the Father of light took six days to complete his task and then he rested on the seventh day. There are many lessons to learn from this but the one that is important and relevant to me now is the fact that everything takes time to accomplish and establish.

We have all heard time and time again that the longest journey begins with the first step. A king is born. Go forth and act. Find that thing that you love to do and do it well. Do it will all your might and soon you will be where you want to be. Again, take all disappointments and set backs as lessons. Use them to propel you forward. Every mistake should make you stronger. Use time as one of your masters because everything takes time. Also everything has it seasons. There is a time to plant and a time to reap. You don't have to be the best planter but be the best planter you can be. Do it right and your success will come. Life is like a dance because in a dance you loose yourself to the moves. You relax yourself to the point that wherever your mind sends your body it will follow.

Life is like a dance. You cannot play football in the spirit of cricket or dance in the spirit playing chess. Everything has its own spirit. When you perform your body and mind must be in the spirit of what you are doing. It is in feeling the music that the dancers connect their minds and bodies and then perform. It is feeling the spirit of the game that famous footballers perform their moments of magic. In the spirit of the game you can live in the heavens. You can reach that level where everything is possible. When "the everything is possible" feeling takes over your body you are a king. Let the beat control your body.

The Everything is Possible Feeling Took Me Over.

I was neither the greatest footballer nor the most loved by any means playing football in the park. I however have some very unforgettable memories. I remembered playing for the Backroad All Stars Team in the community where I grew up. In one particular game, we were down one nil with five minutes remaining in the game when we got a free kick about three feet away from the corner flag. I spotted the ball and looked at my tallest teammate. I delivered the perfect kick for him to score the perfect goal when one of my other teammates rose up and pushed him in the back and he fell. Although he made contact with the ball it went just wide of the post. About two minutes later after pressuring the team, because we needed a draw to go through to next round, we got a corner. The manager said to me please score this one. At that moment the "Everything is possible feeling" took me over. All I could say to him was "The time is now." I spotted the ball and delivered another perfect kick straight to my target who headed the ball pass the goalkeeper. There was a huge celebration and everyone ran to the goal scorer in jubilation. What was good was that I gave the father of light the praises and then the goal scorer came to me and gave me a hug.

There was another experience that will stay with me forever. I was playing another game on the same field playing for this same team. It was the semi-finals and the game ended nil all after extra time. I was not the strongest and fittest player so I was taken off the field. It was time for the penalty shoot out so the team gathered. Again I felt the "Everything is possible" feelings taking me over. I then called our goal keeper and said to him "save one and we will win." The goalkeeper was also immediately taken over by this feeling. He knocked my fist and said, "My name is Chilovert." To be honest, we scored all our penalty shots and our goalkeeper saved all our opponent's penalties. He practically flew like a bird in the goal. At the end after all the celebration, I praised the Father of Light.

Your Relationship with The Father of Light.

I am impressed with an ancient king called David. He was a very good king. He had very humble beginnings just like I did. Like all men he had his strength and weaknesses. King David's weakness was women. This was not a problem for him but the problem came about when he had an affair with one of his key soldier's wife. Realising that the lady was pregnant, he called the soldier from battle and in a nice way gave him the opportunity to spend some time with his wife. In the morning king David had a meeting with his soldier. He asked the soldier in a decoy way "did you have a good time with your wife last night'? The soldier replied "I was not happy because I could not cope with the fact that my colleagues were in a battle and I was enjoying my wife. King David now grew sad because he knew now that he had to do something tragic. He later sent the soldier to the front of the battle and he got killed. A prophet then went to see David and told him a story. The prophet asked him "If a man who had several sheep took away a man's only sheep and killed him, what should happen to this man'? King David replied "That man should be hanged by his tongue." The prophet replied "Thou art that man." At this point King David realised what was happening. This did not go down very well with his people and they were angry with him. King David replied "This is not between me and man, this is between the Father of Light and me" The king went and sought forgiveness for his wrongs.

There are many lessons that can be learned from this story. I was very surprised back by the fact that he said "This is between the Father of Light and me." Your relationship between the Father of Light and you should be personal. This is your life, live it to the fullest. Don't walk around under pressures of guilt. You can relieve yourself from all the pressures and live and be free. The father of light has given us the authority to free ourselves from all the wrongs that we have done. It is important that we acknowledge when we are wrong and move on. We don't even have to acknowledge our wrong to anyone. This can be done just between the father of light and you. A king is born. You may make serious mistakes and you will have to face public scrutiny, but through this phase remember this is not for you and the public. Don't let the public use its judgement to tear you down. Do your own assessment, seek the father of light and move on. Lift yourself above your failures and short comings and the world will see your example, learn from it and gain strength from it. A king is born. Your reaction is important. It is the key to your survival. Crucial situations will come but what is important is how you react to these situations. Rise to the occasion. Gain strength from the father of light and move on even stronger than before.

Count All Your Success

Have you ever wondered why some people are so sad? For some strange reason there seems to be no happiness in their lives. A king is born. You should have a vision for your life. This will give you a reason to live. While you seek to accomplish the task of turning your vision into reality, it is important that you celebrate every success. Have gratitude. I have seen many successful people with success boxes and jars in their house. Each day as they achieve something new, they write it on a piece of paper and store it in their success box. Counting your success as blessing is as good as eating healthy food or as good as doing exercise. While healthy food and exercise strengthens the body, counting your blessings strengthens the mind. If you should stop everyday and count the number of successes that you have had throughout the day, you would be surprised to see the amount of progress that you have made in your life. It is through identifying and celebrating these successes that more success will be come.

We must bear in mind that success breeds success. Let counting your successes a part of your daily routine. The last thing that you should do before you retire at nights is to check your success box and give thanks to the Father of Light. Some people like to look at their gold coins but look at your blessings both tangible and intangible, count them and feel happy about them and then go off to bed feeling happy. A king is born. You will realize that everyday you will wake up feeling happy and ready to go forward to face your new challenge and to come home victorious. This practice, if continued long enough will become a part of your nature. You will eventually realise that your life has become one of gratitude and one of thanksgiving. Some people, no matter what is done for them, it is never enough. They don't perpetuate a life of giving thanks and showing appreciation.

Give thanks for the sunshine, give thanks for the rain, and give thanks for the snow because we might not see them again. In a month's time, after you have started your success box, you will see how much you have accomplish and in one year's time you will be entirely surprise to see the progress that you have made. Whenever you are feeling down, this will be your go to box. Just open it and look at all the blessings that you have gotten so far throughout the year. This will give you something to be happy about. It is this positivity that will motivate you to go forward again and achieve more. Rather than spending your time mauling over the negative happenings in your life, count your blessings. You are a king. Have you ever stopped to think what motivates a man to be a king? He counts his blessings. While you are focussing on his mistakes, he is focussing on his success. You spend all your life talking about his failures and disappointments while he is moving forward with his successes. This is what motivates a man to be king, success.

No procrastination. Have you ever gotten up in the morning and looked at the time and realised that it is time to wake up. Although you know that it is time to get up getting up you decide to take another five minutes to cuddle in the bed. When you wake up after the five minutes you then decide to take another five minutes until these five minutes turn into one hour. You will now be late for work. Procrastinating that will steal your life away. Wake up and go. Today is the day that you will make more successes to store in your box. Today is a gift. Take it with gratitude. Appreciate it and at the end of it count every blessing. A King is born. You are blessed. Your cup is full and running over. People who used to criticise you are now coming to seek you for help and guidance. My cup is full and running over.

A king is born. You are a King only if you start counting those successes today.

How do you feel when nobody comes to you asking for help? Do you still feel valued? I am sure you don't. It is the degree to which we are able to help and serve others that makes us feel valued. The more you achieve for yourself is the more you will attract the mass. People will only come to you for help if they know that you have been there and done that. Achieve, achieve, and achieve. I cannot emphasise the importance of this. Do it even for the joke of it. Even if you don't see the immediate importance of achieving something, as long as the possibility and opportunity is there for you to achieve, go forth and do it. Make yourself a person who knows all things are possible. Create a life full of success. It is these successes that make you a King. Put yourself in a position to help those around you. Support them like your life depends on it. It is in helping others to the top that your top will seem higher than the sky. They will raise you higher. Every time you raise someone they will raise you higher. Keep doing this to as many people as you can and you will be sent to the heavens. A king is born.

Colour Yourself

Do all the good that you can do to all the people you can. This must include you. You must do all the good you can to yourself. The greatest good you can do for yourself is to colour yourself. You must try to achieve all the possible accolades you can throughout your lifetime. Create your own world of glory. Don't wait on others to give you glory. You need to create opportunities for your own good. The more accolades you have, the more you get closer to the father of light. Remember a man's life was given to him for the purpose of expression and that a man expresses himself by way of his achievements in life. Have you ever gone to an event and the introduction of the guest speaker was longer than the guest speaker's speech. The amount of accolades that the guest speaker had achieved could not be talked about in the introduction. Colour yourself. If you work for an organisation and they expect you to achieve a desired quota, as their goal, don't just settle to achieve what they asked you to achieve but endeavour to surpass their expectation. If they give you the task of achieving five, aim to achieving ten. This will colour you. The more colour you have or the more stripes you have, the more you are a king. A king is born. Open your eyes and look around. There are opportunities all around. If you have the courage to colour yourself, this can be achieved with little effort as long as you take the right path and get the right support. Look around you to see how other people created their own world of success and glory. Do they have more power than you or do they have more brain than you? No, but what they might have is a creative energy and drive that they use.

Some people take the right approach to life. They go out to the right places and they meet the right people. If you always hang out with the wrong crowd you will always end up with the wrong badge on your shoulder. This is not good colour for you. The influences of peers are very powerful. It is like training your muscle. The more weight you try to lift, your muscle will grow to adapt to the weights. Socialise with the right crowd. Colour yourself. Make yourself be known. The world is a small village. It has become so small by the introduction of the Information Age. With technology, especially the internet, you have the world right in front of you. Everything is at the touch of a button. Make yourself known to the world. Write your song so that the world can sing it. Play your music so that the world can dance to it. Write your poems so the world can listen to them.

Write your books so the world can read them. Make yourself be known to the world.

The world is your place. Live in it and excel. Don't just be another man but be the man that will be remembered long after you have passed. Leave your mark and your impression on the world. Shake the building. When you walk into a room, your presence must be felt. Have the shaking effect of a massive earthquake. Leave your mark at all times. When you speak, people must listen and when you don't speak they shall thirst and wait anxiously to hear your voice. A single sentence must be like food to them, and from that they shall find strength to be kings. A king is born. If you teach a man how to fish, you might not have to give him a fish again. He will go and fish and bring fish to you his teacher. Speak so that that the mass will prosper and be blessed and the blessing from them shall be upon your shoulder and you children's shoulder. A king is born. You are a king. Rise to the occasion, look at yourself and say that you are strong because when you speak to your mind it will respond accordingly and when it does you will set your body on fire and this fire will light the world. Colour yourself. I have some very high profile cousins. During the reign of Ben Johnson I have a cousin that defeated him in a sprint race. I have another cousin that played for the national football team at a young age.

I also have a cousin that captain the national football team. I have lost a cousin through idleness. He and his friends went to swim in a community pond. They were playing what is called 'sea lick' this is where you use your foot to hit someone in the water as you swim past them. The idea is for you to dive to try to avoid being hit. Unfortunately for my cousin he got hit in the head and when he was struggling some hit him in the head again. He was really getting unconscious but they did not realise this and everyone came and hit him in the head again and again. By the time they realised that he was drowning it was too late and so they run away and leave him to drown. The saying of the dark one comes to mind 'when a man is down keep him down'. Surly this must be a thought from the darkest of the dark. That is what exactly took place. This cousin that I lost was destining for greatness. He was a very good athlete. He was the fastest boy in his age group in school and he was the best footballer in the school. The world lost a king. Idle jesting I learnt from an early age is not good and for that reason when we play, we must play with rules and play with people who will abide by the rules. In an effort to colour yourself you must also protect yourself. For many argue up to this day that the reason my cousin died was because he was so good in what he did that the group of boys wanted to get a chance to hit him even when he was struggling because he was so good they seize the opportunity to hit him at that time for before it would have been almost impossible to get him. I always remember too that the father of the dark is always putting stuff in your way he is always reaching out to you. This is why it is easy to do wrong. Because you don't have to thing to do wrong the father of the dark will put these wrong doing in your way constantly. He parades your thoughts perpetually. He is this loud voice that is always shouting out to you. He is always dress in bright colours you cannot miss him. He is profound. Conversely the father of light is the still small voice. The one you have to reach out to. Reach out to this small voice heed to its words and be one with the light. A king is born.

LET THE BIRD PITCH ON YOUR SHOULDER

If you had the choice between a man who completes a marathon and look weary and tired or a man who completes a marathon and looks very relaxed as if he could run another marathon immediately I am sure that you would want to be the latter. Train yourself so that you look and appear as cool as a cucumber. Even when a situation gets very tense, you should not get tense but you should be as relaxed as possible. Let the dove pitch on your shoulder. Be in complete harmony with nature. Is not an easy feat but when achieved thou will be a King. I am sure that you are already aware of various forms of exercise such as yoga and meditation. Gain control of your mind and body. This is very important for your own good. Why do birds fly and dogs don't fly? Birds are made with wings and in their wings they express that oneness with the air. It is this relaxation and oneness with nature that causes them to fly. When you go bed at night and you dream that you are flying, that is a true sign that you are relaxed. You are living in accordance with nature your mind and body is under your control. Let the dove pitch on your shoulder. I am sure that if you have one hundred birds pitching on you this would be very annoying, but if you have one bird pitched on you how marvellous this would feel. This is a feeling of divinity. This is showing that you are one with nature. Be one with nature and draw close to the father of light. People often speak of a balance diet. But having a balance mind is evermore so important. We know that negative and positive is always going to be in the world and that the two has their place in your life for some reason or the other. It is important to balance them both. It is striking the right balance that will make the bird pitch on your shoulder. When you look at people who excel to the heights of heights they seem to possess something new and different they have this glow this outer circle of energy. They are encircled with and outer layer of power. It is difficult for someone to break through their power zone and get through to them they are so protected. This outer energy is the power of balance. When you entire being is balance you become one with father of light. When you are balance properly you can walk on a rope across a river with gushing waves. Find the proportion of what make you balance. Find the direct proportion of everything you do, how much sleep you need to how many hours of staying up for example, how many carbohydrates to how many proteins and so on. Take the time out to discover your balance. Find out how much exercise you need to keep your physical body balance with your mental body. For when you achieve this level of balance you will literally float on air. You will fly like a bird in the midnight sky. Accidentally and intentionally become one with your situation, your position, your place where you are feeling safe and secure. All the time in your mind maintain that you are safe you are protected by the light and nothing will harm you even if they try to. I am safe I am one with the father of light. Be one with the air you breathe be as calm and gently and feel the air rushes through your lungs and feeding your entire body. Feel your body growing the way you want it to grow. If you want to lose weight feel the weight being lost every second every time you breathe. Feel things going your way and live with this feeling and be relaxed about it. Maintaining your balance should be done effortlessly. For it is whatever we do with least effort will make effect on the mental side of our life. Nothing that is required to be done mentally should be done in stress and struggle. As long as we plant the seed in our conscious mind the subconscious mind will run a million miles with it in a minute. The more relax we are about it the quicker the race will be ran. Be effortless in all mental activities all you need is just the plant of a thought seed. No muscle is required. Just plant the thought and that is it. A king is born I can plant a thought seed and watch it grow into a forest.

HONESTY COUNTS

There was a king a very rich king who had tons of gold and silver. He really loved his precious jewellery. The very sight of gold made him felt powerful and hence happy. He had a very beautiful daughter. When she became an adult and it was time for her to get married, the king was very happy. However, he had one major problem. The problem was that he did not want just any man to marry his beautiful daughter. He wanted someone who was honest. He did not want her to marry someone who wanted her for just her money and glory. He then hosted a party at his palace to find the best candidate. It was a long walk to get up to the palace because the palace was on a hill. The king lined the walkway with lots of gold coins. He then invited all the handsome young men from the country to his party because he said he wanted someone very honest to marry his beautiful daughter. The King made sure that there were no guards placed on the pathway to the palace.

In those days, there were no cameras, therefore it was clear for them to take anything because there was nobody watching them. All the men except one filled their pockets with gold coins. As soon as they entered the palace, the King brought them to the back and showed them a big field. He ordered them to run around the field twice and the winner would marry the princess. When the race started, by the first lap, all except one man was tired and he won the race quite easily. He won very easy because he did not have any weight in his pockets. His pockets were empty. He had no gold coins in his pockets. The rest of the men had gold coins in their pockets so they were heavy and they got tired very easily. The king ordered the winner to take his daughter. A king was born. When you play your cards play them right. Be ever so mindful that when nobody is watching you, you are watching you. You can't run away or you can't hide from yourself. Always remember be good for goodness sake. A king is born.

The Power of the Spoken Word

I leave you with a very important story. A pastor had a lifetime preaching and teaching about the father of light and his power of forgiveness. During one his life long messages, he made several references to the "Blood of Jesus" and that it is able to wash away all our sins and set us free. His entire life as a messenger was based on this divine principle. He preached about it so much that it became a part of him. He was very rich and had five lovely children. There were three beautiful girls and two handsome boys. His three girls Jane, Mary and Sue were very good scholar, and as such, their dad was very proud of them. The two boys also made him very proud because Tom was excellent in Science and Jerry was a Linguist. As a linguist Jerry became and ambassador for his country. The nature of his job meant that he had to do many overseas travels. During his travels to these different countries he got engaged in multiple activities, some professional and some social. He also met several different kinds of people and of course some were professional and some were not.

One day he went to a meeting and he met a beautiful lady. This first meeting was entirely professional as this was in relation to his job. Over time their professional relationship grew very strong until there was a very strong bond between them. They started meeting each other on different occasions and developed a very good chemistry. They eventually started dating each other. After dating for several months, the day finally came when Jerry made his move and asked his lady if she would marry him. The response he got was a big yes. One night while they were talking, she revealed a shocking story to him that she used to be a Pole Dancer. This came really shocking to him because the quality of his lady did not match her unbelievable past. He pondered over the revelation for a long time. During his pondering the chemistry between them however grew stronger and stronger and they became inseparable. They finally decided that they would get married. He however realised that the news would cause a struggle for him and his family, especially with his dad. In addition, as a government official, it would seem disgraceful if it was known that his wife was an ex-pole dancer. This was going to be an uphill task for him, but one that he could not avoid because he was so much in love with his fiancée.

When he went back home with his fiancée, she was loved immediately by all who saw her. Everyone in his family, his community and all the government officials were really excited and happy for him. However, he had something on his mind that worried him. He knew that the day when everyone found out about the unaccepted past of his lady then their happiness would turn into sadness. He knew he had to make it known to them. He then made an announcement that he would have two parties and all his family members, friends and co-workers were invited. He told them that the second party would be a month after. At the first party everyone was excited. They drank wine and champagne and were all absolutely merry. Midway during the party stopped he music and gave a shocking speech about his relationship with his beautiful lady and how deeply in love he was with her. Everyone was appalled but although they were very happy listening to his speech, they were worried because they had never heard him speak like that before. They could sense that something strange was coming. He finally told them that his fiancée was a Pole Dancer. The place got very quiet for about two minutes and then the place erupted in a loud noise and chatterers. The gathering started to disperse as people started to leave the party. Days past and he did not contact parents, friends or co-workers. He finally broke the silent and announced that he and his fiancée would be hosting the second party and everyone was free to come and ask any questions they want to ask.

The idea of the second party was appealing to all and as such everyone was excited and could not wait for the day. There was never a larger gathering in his community because everyone came out to witness the occasion. As usual, all the guests were involved in drinking wine, champagne and merry making. The moment finally arrived and they were asked to sit on the "hot chairs" for questioning. The first question as expected came from his dad and was directed to his lady. He really got straight to the point and asked her to tell everyone about her past. The question came from a man who lived all his life on the principle that the Father of Light is able to cleanse all unrighteousness and set us free. Before the woman could speak and reveal her past to the public who was mad at her Jerry intervened and said "what's on trial today, is it this beautiful lady?' He also replied, "Isn't it that the blood of Jesus can wash away all our sins". The Father of Light can do all things. At this point nobody could speak and there was silence for a long time until his dad asked for the music to restart. The party continued until very late in the night. Two weeks later Jerry married his beautiful fiancée and they lived happily ever after with joy and happiness like every normal couple. A king is born.

Find something to do and enjoy doing it and use your time in doing it well. Make many mistakes and learn from them, do not be put off by your critics. Just keep enjoining what you are doing. A king is born. YOU ARE THAT KING.